ALL THE TEA IN CHINA

ALL THE TEA IN CHINA

By Kit Chow and Ione Kramer

CHINA BOOKS AND PERIODICALS, INC.

SAN FRANCISCO

We would like to thank the following publishers for their kind permission to quote from these copyrighted works: *The Book of Tea*, by Kakuzo Okakura. Dover Publications: New York, 1964. *The Great Tea Venture*, by J. M. Scott. E. P. Dutton, Inc.: New York, 1964. *Chinese Medicinal Herbs*, by Li Shizhen. Translated by F. Porter Smith and G. A. Stuart. Georgetown Press: San Francisco, 1973. Reprinted with permission of the estate of Beatrice Bliss. *To Think of Tea!* by Agnes Repplier. Houghton Mifflin: New York. Copyright © 1932 by Agnes Repplier. Copyright © renewed 1960 by Fidelity Philadelphia Trust Company as executor of the author. Reprinted with permission of Houghton Mifflin Company. Lu Yu's *The Classic of Tea*, translated by Francis Ross Carpenter. English language translation copyright © 1974 by Francis Ross Carpenter. *The Book of Coffee and Tea*, by Joel Schapira. St. Martin's Press, Inc.: New York. Copyright © 1975. *Chinese Herbal Remedies*, by Albert Y. Leung. Universe Books: New York, 1964. Copyright © by Albert Y. Leung. *The Chinese Art of Tea*, by John Blofeld, copyright © 1985. Reprinted by arrangement with Shambhala Publications, Inc., 300 Massachusetts Ave., Boston, MA 02115.

Photo credits: pp. 16, 38, 76 — *China Pictorial*; p. 40 —Grace Tea Company; pp. 54, 56, 58 — Japan National Tourist Organization; pp. 64, 66, 68, 70, 71 — Asian Art Museum (San Francisco); p. 69 — Sharmon Goff; p. 81 — Huang Min Seng; pp. 79, 82, 83, 117, 120 — Chai Bao Tong; pp. 132, 139 — Sibila Savage.

Drawings by Wendy Lee: pp. 5, 11, 25, 32, 52, 61, 72, 80, 131, 159. Illustrations from William Ukers' *All About Tea*: pp. 8, 9, 18, 22, 29, 30, 35.

Cover design by John Heisch
Cover photographs by Sibila Savage
Book design by Janet Wood

Library of Congress Catalog Card Number: 89-60878
ISBN 0-8351-2194-1

Printed in the United States of America by
China Books & Periodicals, Inc.

CHINA
BOOKS
& Periodicals, Inc.

"All the tea in China—" A phrase symbolizing great riches. First used in Australia in the 1890s, according to lexicographer Eric Partridge, as "not for all the tea in China," meaning not at any price.

Contents

Acknowledgments

Every book encompasses the efforts of many people. We want to give special thanks to Professor Chi-Tang Ho of Rutgers University for his advice and encouragement on scientific matters, Dr. Zhang Yichu, Xinhua Hospital, Shanghai Second Medical University, for help with Chinese medical literature and terms. Thanks are due to Zhan Yihou, officer-in-charge of the People's Liberation Army Air Force Retirees' Quarters in Hangzhou, who led co-author Kit Chow on a visit to the Longjing tea plantations and to sample the Lung Ching Tea brewed with Tiger Run Spring water, one of the finest experiences for tourists to Hangzhou. We are also grateful to Zhu Peilian, supervisor of one of the Liuxi tea plantations, who gladly provided information about Liuxi tea, and to Charles Cheung, who presented Kit with Liuxi tea and encouraged him in this project.

Others who deserve special mention are: Tea Master Aiko Tauchi of the Japanese Cultural Center at Foothill College, Los Altos Hills, California, for reading the Japanese portions of the manuscript, and Professor Michiko Hiramatsu, director of the center, for much advice and information; Michael Spillane, President of the G. S. Haly Company, Inc. tea importers of Redwood City, California, for advice and a copy of a videotape on Chinese teas; Lillian Hatton, Director of Consumer Services, Tea Council of the U.S.A., for information and help in many directions; William MacMelville, a long-time member of the tea trade, for help on the Hyson question; Samuel H. G. Twining, Director, R. Twining and Company Ltd., London; and the staffs of many libraries, and that of the library of Mountain View, California, in particular.

Photo-wise our thanks go to David Vardy, proprietor of the Daruma Tearoom in Berkeley, for advice and the loan of his painting of the Zen founder; Xu Duangfeng, of Anxi, Fujian province; Zhu Chengyao of *China Pictorial* magazine in Beijing, China, for help in getting several photos and to the editors of that magazine and of *China Today* (formerly *China Reconstructs*) magazine in Beijing for the use of photos. Very special thanks to Zhang Shuicheng, photographer for *China Today* whose friendship extended to searching for just the right photo with a flashlight through the subterranean chambers of the office where he and Ione once worked together. And thanks to many, many others in China and the United States who contributed to making this book possible.

Thanks also to many members, past and present, of the staff of China Books & Periodicals, including Ms. Nancy Ippolito, Book Division Manager, Foster Stockwell, editor Bob Schildgen, Wesley S. Palmer for initial research on growing and processing, and Chin Chi for initial research on tea history and for kindhearted support in many other ways.

Preface

Many of the things long considered pleasures of life, such as sweets, rich food, alcohol, and smoking have turned out, on closer examination, to be not so good for us. Indulging in them can contribute to high blood pressure, obsesity, heart disease, diabetes, and cancer. Tea, however, is one of those rare treasures, enjoyed throughout the world, that actually benefits health. Tea has been shown to counteract some of the bad effects of our other favorites.

While this may come as a surprise to Westerners, in the Orient it has been known for two thousand years. Long before tea became one of China's main exports, it was a staple of life, creating a fascinating cultural history in China. But the story of procuring and serving it is no less intriguing in other lands which fell in love with the little green leaf, especially Japan, Britain, and Russia.

Knowledge of the benefits of tea is the basis for continuing tea research in China, Japan, and other Asian lands and new investigations in the West. Tea drinking may help avert some of the worst heart diseases, according to Chinese doctors who have studied the subject. Modern scientific research in both East and West has found that regular tea drinking can lower blood fats and prevent cholesterol accumulation. Tea can play an important role in keeping weight down. By stimulating the kidneys and other internal organs, it prevents formation of stones. The effect of tea in preventing the development of cancer is the subject of several current studies.

Stepped-up research on tea's relation to health has led to the use of tea and its derivatives in treating illness. Medicines made from tea are now regularly employed in China to treat hypertension, nephritis, and many other conditions.

Tea research stands at new frontiers and the way ahead is not always clear. Investigators in China and Japan seem eager to prove what they already believe, that tea *is* beneficial. At the other extreme, researchers in the United States and other Western countries take a skeptical view and focus mainly on the dangers of tea. They often begin from the premise that tea is harmful, and concentrate on what they believe to be negative aspects, such as caffeine.

The popular view in the West, with the exception of Britain, is that tea is bad for you. Essentially it reads like this: the less you get of tea's two main components, caffeine and what is known as tannin, the better. Or, if tea is beneficial, it is so mainly by default. For instance, due to concern over caffeine, tea is considered preferable to coffee only because it contains less of that substance.

However, tea not only contains less caffeine than coffee, but according to the most recent research, this substance taken in moderation is perfectly safe for normally healthy people. Those tannins (mistrusted by many because of their confusion with tannic acid, which they are not, see p. 88) turn out to be among the most beneficial substances in tea, as they counteract cholesterol and other blood fats.

Why views on tea should differ so markedly, and what this says about these two great cultural streams, is also not clear. Is it that people in the West have encountered so much substance abuse in recent years that we are suspicious of everything? Or is it that peoples of the West lack sufficient exposure to the riches of the Asian tea tradition to make it theirs? ("I am Chinese. Tea is in my very bones," co-author Kit Chow observed one day in the course of preparing this work.)

In this book we try to bring together these two vastly different traditions, and to make each understandable in terms of the other. We will probably go on discovering, refining, and redefining for some time to come. Some points remain so obscure that they can only be brought into line by further research in China.

We hope that by bringing to the West the story of tea in China, and of Chinese teas and their lore, much of which has never been published in English, more people will begin to leap the cultural gap and share with China this, her discovery—for enjoyment and for health.

Introduction

Better to be deprived of food for
three days than of tea for one.

Ancient Chinese saying

K nown throughout Asia as one of China's great treasures, tea is second only to water as a world beverage. Tea has been linked with health from the very beginning, and is prized for its ability to banish fatigue, stimulate the mental powers, and raise the energy level.

The Taoist philosophers and Buddhist monks, who did much to promote tea and improve its cultivation in China, imbued tea drinking with greater meaning than is applied to any other beverage. Tea drinking does, in fact, reflect much that is characteristically Chinese, from the taste itself to the way it is served. Anyone who has tried to describe the taste of tea will recall having a difficult time. The flavor is much more subtle than that of coffee or chocolate. The man of letters, Lu Yu, who wrote a classic work on tea about which we shall hear more later, spoke of "a haunting flavor, strange and lasting."

The most famous Chinese description of the joys of drinking tea is by Lu Tong, a Tang dynasty (A.D. 618–907) poet famous for his love of tea, entitled "Thanks to Imperial Censor Meng for His Gift of Freshly Picked Tea." The poet tells how this high official sent him some tea, and he retired to prepare it:

The first cup caresses my dry lips and throat,
The second shatters the walls of my lonely sadness,
The third searches the dry rivulets of my soul to find the stories of
   five thousand scrolls.
With the fourth the pain of past injustice vanishes through my
   pores.

The fifth purifies my flesh and bone.
With the sixth I am in touch with the immortals.
The seventh gives such pleasure I can hardly bear.
The fresh wind blows through my wings
As I make my way to Penglai. *

The stimulating effect of tea brings into harmony two seemingly contradictory elements—alertness and relaxation. Lu Yu held that tea was the essence of moderation, and that one should sip it as though it were life itself, never taking more than three cups at a time. An offer of a cup of tea is therefore like an invitation to relax and enjoy the here and now for what it is.

What can be called tea may be made from many plants. Today there are a multitude of herbal teas on the market and indeed herbal teas have always been a tradition in China, more for medical than beverage use. Here we confine the discussion to true tea, made from the leaf of the plant *Camellia sinensis.*

One of the ironies of history is that this "peaceful" drink should have been such an important factor in two revolutions—the American Revolution in 1776 and the modern Chinese Revolution, China's long struggle against foreign imperialism, which began with the Opium Wars of 1840 and 1857 and finally ended in the creation of a new China in 1949.

In the American Revolution the beverage led to the Boston Tea Party on December 16, 1773, when three shiploads of tea chests were dumped into Boston harbor. The American colonists regarded the tax on tea as a symbol for many edicts Britain had imposed on the colonies without consulting them.

The Opium War grew out of the drain on Britain's silver supply as Chinese tea gained popularity in nineteenth century England. To recoup the silver that was being sent to China to purchase tea, opium was sold to China. Chinese action against opium importation brought retaliation from Britain and the Opium War which forced China to legalize sales of the drug.

---

* Mt. Penglai, off the coast of Shandong province, was the traditional home of the immortals.

China's tea trade reached its peak in 1886, but her economy was already in a general decline as a result of unsettled conditions created by the Opium War and the Taiping Rebellion. Indian and Ceylon teas began driving Chinese tea off the world market in the 1860s. By the 1940s India and Japan were the main tea exporters.

Today China's production and trade are on the rebound. In 1949 the country that gave tea to the world produced only 4,000 tons of it. By 1985, output of processed tea was nearly 440,000 tons and by 1988, 545,000 tons. Exports went up from 137,000 tons in 1985 to 197,000 in 1988 and 203,000 in 1989. Tea is China's most valuable agricultural export, earning $400 million in 1989, and her third largest export commodity after grain and silk.

China's biggest markets (1985 figures) are in order: Morocco (18,668 tons), United States, Tunisia, Poland, Hongkong, Soviet Union, and United Kingdom. The developing nations are becoming increasingly important tea buyers, taking 35 percent of China's exports.

Now China's second largest customer, the United States doubled its tea purchases from China between 1978 and 1983 as normalization of relations between the two countries proceeded. Sales of Chinese tea to the United States continue to rise, going up from 12,574 tons in 1985

1982	China's production surpasses previous high set in 1914
1984	Exports surpass previous high set in 1886
1985	China tops Sri Lanka to become third in world tea exports
	China National Tea Import and Export Corporation set up, a marketing company solely for tea
1986	China tops Sri Lanka to become second world producer

Some Milestones

---

to 20,000 in 1988. This increase has played a large role in China's regaining her place in the world market. In 1977 tea from China accounted for only three percent of the tea imports to both the United States and the United Kingdom. Recently China has supplied 16 percent of U.S. imports and 7.7 percent (1984) of Britain's.

Tea drinking has been gaining popularity in the United States in recent years. Tea has been described in various publications as "the newest chic, a more gracious way to do business than the power breakfast, a quiet revolution . . . as people switch from alcohol to tea, from standing in noisy, crowded bars to sitting in spacious, refined tearooms."

Most of the best hotels have tearooms, often serving the beverage with British style delicacies. They have also appeared on the streets of many communities, and we were surprised to find a complete line of teas served in an ordinary Cupertino, California eatery of the type that years back would not have thought of tea. U.S. consumption exceeds 50 billion cups a year.

ONE 🌿 *China: The Tea Tradition*

F irst, how did tea come to be?

Its origin as a beverage is lost in antiquity, but Chinese legend provides an answer, saying that tea was discovered accidentally about 3000 B.C. by Shen Nong, the Divine Cultivator. Also credited with inventing agriculture and herbal medicine, he is honored as one of China's three mythical early sovereigns. One day leaves of the tea plant fell into water he was boiling outdoors. He liked the drink, found it to have medicinal value, and tea was born. Another legend says that as an experimental herbalist he sampled various kinds of plants to determine

Shen Nong, the Divine Cultivator, who is credited with discovering tea, teaching the people to farm. From a Yuan dynasty tomb carving.

1

their individual effects. This boldness sometimes resulted in poisoning, and he used tea as an antidote.

A legend of a much later date, from Japan, concerns Bodhidharma, or Dharuma, the Indian monk who brought Zen Buddhism to China in A.D. 520. The emperor gave him a cave-temple outside the capital, Nanjing, where he proceeded to demonstrate the benefits of meditation, a strong point of Zen (the name Zen, or *chan* in Chinese, comes from the Sanskrit word for meditation). Bodhidharma meditated for nine years while staring at a wall.

Once he fell asleep. To make sure that his eyelids did not droop again, he cut them off and cast them away. Where they fell a plant grew, the tea plant, from whose leaves a drink can be prepared which drives away sleep. The aid of tea during long hours of meditation may indeed explain how monks became instrumental in spreading its fame. Later Zen monks took to honoring their founder by sipping tea before a statue of him.

At any rate, the leaves were first plucked from the wild plant, which was later cultivated. This latter step may have begun in China's southwestern province of Sichuan and then moved down the valley of the Yangtze River.

Dharuma is always portrayed without eyelids, which went to create tea plants. From a painting by Shuha.

BACK TO CENTURY MINUS-TWELVE

Chinese historical research has found evidence of the use of tea much earlier than was once thought. As far back as the twelfth century B.C., King Wen, founder of the Zhou dynasty, is said to have received tea as tribute from the tribal heads in and around present-day Sichuan. This is mentioned in a book written about these areas shortly after A.D. 347, *Treatise on the Kingdom of Huayang* by Chang Ju. Until the third century B.C. the fresh leaves were boiled with water. Drying and processing of the leaves began around that time as tea became a daily beverage.

The celebrated third century surgeon Hua Tuo, originator of anesthesia, is reported as saying that tea drinking increased concentration and alertness. Liu Kun, a top general in the Qin dynasty (221–206 B.C.) serving as governor in Yanzhou (Shandong), wrote his nephew that he was feeling old and depressed, and to send some "real tea." A 59 B.C. book by Wang Bao tells how to buy and brew tea in Wuyang, now Pengshan, in central Sichuan province. China's oldest medical book, *Shen Nong's Canon of Medicinal Herbs* (a collection of herbal remedies first compiled around A.D. 500) includes mentions of tea.

By A.D. 350, the beverage was well enough known to be included in an addition in that year to the *Erya* encyclopedia-dictionary originally published six hundred years earlier. It is described as a drink made by boiling the leaves of the tea plant.

Early references used a character pronounced *tu*, which also refers to the sow-thistle. To distinguish the two, a Han dynasty emperor ruled that this character be pronounced *cha* when referring to tea. In the eighth century one bar disappeared from the middle vertical stroke, giving *cha* a character all its own.

During the fifth century, tea drinking spread rapidly in the south and more slowly in the north. By then tea was well established as a beverage. A Jin dynasty poet wrote, "Fragrant tea superimposes the six passions; the taste for it spreads over the nine districts (meaning the whole country)." Tea was sent to the emperors of the Eastern Jin dynasty (317–420). It must have already been taken up by some of the nomadic tribes, for Chinese records note its use in barter trade with Turkic peoples in A.D. 476.

In the far reaches, tea pressed into cakes served as a medium of exchange almost from the beginning of the tea trade. Tea cakes continued in this role even after paper money was introduced in the eleventh century. Tea merchants were responsible for the first bank drafts in the Tang dynasty. They found it difficult and dangerous to carry the gold payment for their sales back to the south from the capital Chang'an (today's Xi'an). So provincial representatives in the capital, who had to turn in certain sums to the crown each year, used the gold from tea sales for this purpose and wrote drafts entitling the merchants to collect their proceeds on their return to the provinces.

Tea got its own character in the Tang dynasty.

TANG: FOR TEA TOO, A GOLDEN AGE

In the Tang dynasty (618–907), tea drinking became an art. One of China's golden ages, this was also the golden age of tea drinking, often done with elaborate ritual. The Chinese empire was the largest on earth. Caravans from the Middle East came for China's beautiful and unique silks and porcelains. They also came for tea. In the centuries that followed, the use of tea from China spread throughout an area stretching from Mongolia to the Caspian Sea.

Tea from Yangxian, located in mountains straddling the Jiangsu-Zhejiang provincial border, was praised by Lu Yu and considered best. Late in the eighth century, some given to a visiting official reached the emperor, who then demanded that a quantity be sent every year. Although tea had been presented to emperors for centuries (one Anhui county has records of regular deliveries in the years 317–312), with this Yangxian incident tea is held to have joined the regular list of tribute products expected from every locality growing it.

Picking tribute tea became a festival in early spring, with thousands of young women gathering early in the morning on the mountains. In some areas, local people invited monks to burn incense and recite scriptures before tea picking. The ritual was usually led by the clan's seniors or a magistrate. After the proper ceremonies, the young women picked till noon, and the leaves were processed by men before the day ended. For the latter, designated towns set up special wine shops and "pleasure girl" establishments for the occasion. But being forced during the busy plowing time to give labor at very low pay—much of which was lost in such pleasures—was a hardship for the peasants.

This tribute, sent ostensibly as a gift or sign of loyalty to the emperor, amounted to a tax, and became a heavy burden on the peasants. All emperors down till the end of the Qing dynasty in 1911 collected such tribute. Some of it found its way abroad in state foreign trade.

The bright side is that the use of these products by the court, imperial relatives, and high officials, stimulated a demand for more and fostered the internal economy. The sale of tea in China and later the foreign tea trade brought revenue to cash-poor rural areas. A large transport industry developed, and one for the production of the wooden chests in which the tea was sold. As tea drinking spread, the desire for fine porcelain for the tea service was a spur to the ceramics industry.

In the thirteenth century, tea drinking forced the growth of the silk industry in the north. Tea became so popular among all classes there that purchases of it caused severe drain on the northern economy, much as was to happen with Britain in the eighteenth century. Unsuccessful at limiting consumption to officials above a certain rank, the court decided to produce more silk in the north to pay for the tea.

Tea played a role in China's relations with the peoples of her frontier regions. In Tang times, tea drinking spread rapidly among the Mongol, Tartar, Turkic, and Tibetan nomadic peoples living on the northwestern and western frontiers. They found that tea taken in large quantities helped remedy ills rising from the lack of vegetables and fruit in their diet, which consisted mainly of meat and milk products. Tea soon became an essential for the nomads, and often a factor in their maintaining some kind of peaceful relations with the dynastic government in order to carry on barter trade.

Traditional depiction of Lu Yu.

LU YU AND THE TEA CLASSIC

The Tang dynasty saw the first comprehensive treatise on tea and its varieties, though shorter works had appeared earlier. This was *The Book of Tea* (Cha Jing) now known as *The Classic of Tea* by the man of letters Lu Yu (733–804). Little is known about his antecedents except that he was a native of Hunan province. Apparently abandoned on a riverbank when he was very small, he was found and adopted by the famed Buddhist monk, Ji Ji, of the Dragon Cloud Buddhist monastery. Ji gave the boy the name Lu Yu, obtained from the Taoist classic *The Book of Changes* (I Ching).

Lu did not want to become a monk so was put to tending a herd of buffalo. What is probably a Confucian retelling of his story has him so avid for study that he practiced writing his characters while sitting astride a buffalo. If you see a figurine or painting of such a one, it is probably him.

Later he became a clown with a group of traveling performers and endeared himself to the company for his cutting and editing of play texts. After years of wandering he settled in Zhejiang province. Lu's interest in tea dated back to those early years when he had to brew it for his foster father. Tea drinking had become widespread and Lu began to investigate the process and its history. The tea growers wanted a systematic codification of tea information. He began work in 760 and the book was published in 780.

The chapter headings are:

1. Origin, Characteristics, Names, and Qualities of Tea.
2. Tools for Plucking and Processing Tea.
3. Varieties, Plucking and Processing Methods.
4. Utensils for Making and Drinking Tea.
5. Methods of Making Tea and the Water of Various Places.
6. Habits of Tea Drinking.
7. Stories, Plantations and Tea as a Medicine.
8. Which Kinds of Tea Are Better in Different Locations.
9. Utensils Which May Be Omitted.
10. How to Copy This Book on Silk Scrolls.

The book made Lu a celebrity. He spent the last decades of his long life in semi-seclusion polishing others of his total of ten books, all now lost. Lu Yu's work played a great role in giving tea cultural significance, Francis Ross Carpenter points out in the preface to his translation of *The Classic of Tea*. Before Lu Yu, tea was a rather ordinary drink, says an early preface to the classic, and "he taught us to manufacture tea, to lay out the equipage and to brew it properly."

After Lu became known as the patron saint of tea, tales about him proliferated. The water used for tea is crucial and Lu was skilled at distinguishing its kinds. He later wrote a book on twenty sources for fine water, the best of which was held to come from midstream on the Yangtze at Nanling. Water from near the bank was often brackish. During a trip on the river his host gave Lu water from that spot to taste. Lu sipped and said the water was from near the bank. The servant who

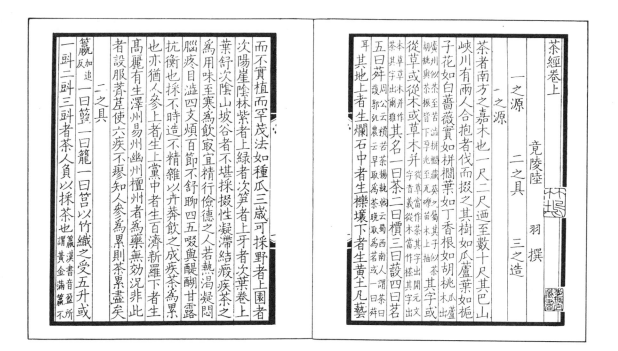

In another tale, the emperor refused to believe the story that when Lu left home his foster father gave up tea because no one could make it so well. The emperor invited the old abbot to the palace for a cup of tea made by his most skilled court lady. The monk was not impressed. But, when served a cup of another brew, he declared that even his son could not do better. What the abbot did not know is that the second cup had been made by Lu himself, summoned to the palace to make tea for an "unknown guest."

Contests testing their acuity at tasting were a popular pastime among officials in both the Tang and subsequent Song dynasties. Participants

The first page of **The Classic of Tea**.

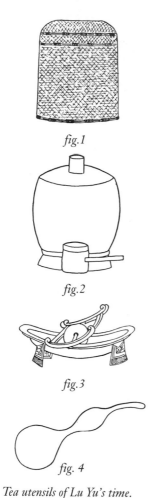

fig.1

fig.2

fig.3

fig. 4

Tea utensils of Lu Yu's time.
1. *Bamboo basket for firing.*
2. *Wooden form and iron mallet for pounding tea into cakes.* 3. *Roller for crushing brick tea.* 4. *Water ladle.*

would nominate a judge, and each in turn prepared a tea of his choice for the others to identify. Greatest taster of them all was probably Cai Xiang, born in 1012. Many tales are told about this native of Fujian province who served as its tea commissioner and later governor, including his role in building a bridge at the town of Chuanzhou. He was able, one story says, to tell when even a tiny bit of a cheaper tea had been added to make a cup of the expensive Small Rounds (two ounces of gold for a little over a pound). His *Tea Record* (Cha Lu), a report to the emperor, is another renowned tea book.

SONG AND THE 'TEA EMPEROR'

Greater farm productivity in the subsequent Song dynasty (960–1279) allowed for more subsidiary crops. Thus it was possible for tea to move from the role of luxury to that of necessity, even among the poorest households. A contemporary writer describes night markets in the Northern Song capital, Kaifeng, running through the third watch (3:00–5:00 a.m.) with vendors bringing in their jars of tea all the while.

The Southern Song capital, Hangzhou, the world's greatest city of its time, had numerous teahouses also serving soups and seasonal snacks. They featured flower arrangements according to season and displayed works of prominent painters on the walls. In some, young men of wealthy families gathered, in others, domestic servants, laborers and artisans of different trades. The reason for going to a teahouse, says one account, had nothing to do with tea, which was only an excuse. Young men gathered to play instruments or sing, and enjoy the performances or the company.

Among the wealthy, tea drinking as an art rose to new heights, and a small teahouse was included in many of the beautiful gardens that officials built. The first Song emperor received brick tea in gold boxes as tribute, and Hui Zong (r. 1100–1125), its last to function fully, wrote an exhaustive treatise on Song tea. He was patron of a search that found several new varieties.

Hui Zong was noted for his extravagance in pleasing Li Shishi, one of the famous courtesans of Chinese history, who became his concubine. Meanwhile extortions and high taxes from his officials wrecked the economy and led to two of China's greatest peasant revolts. Yet Hui Zong, himself a poet, was a patron of literature and painting. It appears that he even made tea himself, certainly unusual for an emperor. His descriptions in his *Treatise on Tea* (Da Guan Cha Lun, 1107) show a remarkable mastery of the details of tea production. These, along with the Song gentleman's feeling for tea, he recorded for posterity.

He finally abdicated in favor of his son, but the Nuzhen Tartars, who had set up the Jin dynasty in the north, invaded the capital Kaifeng and carried both to captivity beyond the Great Wall. The prisoners remained there for the rest of their lives.

fig. 5

fig. 6

fig. 7

fig. 8

STYLES THROUGH HISTORY

The tea we have been talking about so far was green tea sold in cakes made of the leaves steamed, crushed, fired, pounded and compressed. In Lu Yu's time, a bit was broken off, roasted until, in his words, it was "soft as a baby's arm" and boiled in a pot of water.

The main tea styles in Chinese history, all green tea, can be roughly summarized as follows: early days, fresh leaves boiled in water; third century on, leaves dried and powdered, then boiled; Tang, brick tea, made from leaves steamed, powdered, formed into cakes, and boiled before drinking; Song, dry tea leaves ground to a powder and whipped in hot water with a fine bamboo whisk (this practice was taken to Japan in the eighth or ninth century and is still followed in the tea ceremony there); Ming, loose tea much like ours today and prepared by infusion in hot water. Early in the Song dynasty the drink was enlivened by the addition of onions, pickle juice, ginger, and orange peel. Later it was drunk clear.

Trade with the peoples on the fringes of the empire had grown increasingly important by Song times. Brick tea had been bartered for horses from the steppes, but now it was used to control the nomads— by withholding their annual quota if they became too warlike. To ensure

5. Sieves for sifting crushed leaves. 6. Brush for removing dust. 7. Lacquer cup holder to protect hands from heat. 8. Bamboo brush for washing pots.

enough tea stock to barter for horses the army needed, the Song government prohibited all officials below the rank of seventh grade from purchasing it. Tea remained one of the main commodities exchanged for horses and wool up to 1949 and the establishment of the People's Republic.

Song ceramics, widely used as tea accessories, rank among China's most beautiful arts. Tea had formerly been drunk out of small bowls. Now wide, shallow vessels rather like saucers *(chen)* were used. Song connoisseurs preferred tea that whipped up to a whitish, milky mixture. Black ceramics were favored for the contrast they provided. Spoons of gold, silver, iron, or bamboo were used to drop the leaves into the water. In general, however, the tea masters disapproved of metal.

The conquest of China by the Mongols from the north went on from the late thirteenth century up until the demise of their rule in 1368. It is strange that Marco Polo's *Travels,* which gave detailed descriptions of life in China in 1271–1294 during the rule of Kublai Khan, mentioned tea only in passing, although subsequent Western visitors remarked on it. Polo did say that in 1285 a finance minister had been reprimanded for enforcing the tea tax too ruthlessly.

Chinese sources provide information on numerous teahouses in the city of Hangzhou during the exact time Polo visited it, and surely the Mongols, like most border peoples, must have used tea before coming to the capital. One explanation for Polo's silence may be that he considered tea a custom of the people Kublai had conquered, and therefore not worthy of mention.

Mongol rule was overthrown by the Ming dynasty in 1368. The Ming monarchs, who were from China's majority Han people, sought to revive past glories and customs, including tea drinking. The Horse and Tea Bureau played a vital role in the Ming economy. The demand for the product by the border peoples had become so great that tea ranked as a major commodity significant to the empire both militarily and financially. The bureau, responsible for bartering tea for horses, was headed by a very high official. As an incentive to grow tea in sufficient quantities, the tax was returned to the moderate amount levied at its beginning in the Tang dynasty.

As an art, tea drinking in Ming followed Song traditions, with connoisseurs sipping it delicately in accordance with the maxim "Tea should be

Ming dynasty officials at tea.

drunk often but in small quantities." Meanwhile, great progress was made in the manufacture of ceramic tea sets, and the teapot became the ideal vessel for brewing tea. Shallow drinking bowls remained the custom. Only much later were these transformed into cups.

Door-to-door tea vendors, Yuan dynasty. Outline drawing after Yuan dynasty painting by Zhao Mengfu (1254–1322).

TWO ❧ *Tea Goes to the World*

Japan was among the earliest countries to be deeply influenced by China's tea drinking, which was one of the many customs to spread from China to Japan during the Tang dynasty. Japanese history records that as early as 729 Emperor Shomu served tea to a hundred monks in the palace. The Japanese surmise that the leaves had been brought back by their missions to China.

Buddhists in China had been tea drinkers for a long time, as it helped them stay awake during their long meditations. In 803 the Japanese Buddhist monk Saicho (posthumously known as Dengyo Daishi) went to study in China and there met another Japanese monk, Eichu. They came home together in 805, the former bringing tea seeds, which he planted in a monastery. Five years later, after the plant had reached maturity, Emperor Saga stopped at the monastery and Eichu, its abbot, served him green tea he had processed. The emperor enjoyed it so much that he instituted tea cultivation in five provinces near the capital. Tea was to become an important part of Japanese life.

The original Japanese tea ceremony began as a custom practiced in China during the Tang dynasty. However, while it died out in China, the Japanese continued developing it as a complex ritual with close ties to art. Japanese artists designed beautiful bowls, jars, cups, incense burners, and other utensils for the ceremony.

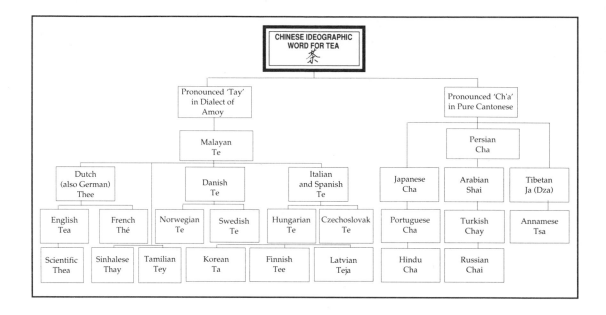

Probable etymological derivation of the word 'tea' in various languages from chart by William Ukers.

TO EUROPE WITH THE DUTCH

The first tea reached Europe around 1610 on Dutch ships from Java, where they picked up tea transported from China by Chinese vessels. The Dutch had come to Java in 1596 and established a transshipment depot for products from the Orient. There they could have met Chinese traders from Fujian and learned the Fukienese name *te*. In 1602 the Dutch East India Company was formed to regulate trade among competing ships, and in that same year the first Dutch vessel sailed into Japan. It seems quite likely that some Chinese and Japanese tea, at least as a curiosity, was taken back to Europe. The value of tea as a commodity must have been recognized by 1610, for Dutch ships carried some from Macao to Java.

By 1637 the company's directors were writing their governor-general in Java: "As tea begins to come into use by some of the people, we expect some jars of Chinese as well as Japanese tea with each ship." This was green tea. Black tea did not replace it till the mid-eighteenth century.

Within a few years, tea had become very popular in Dutch high society. It was extremely expensive and sold in medicine shops. By 1675 it was available in food stores and was in general use throughout Holland. Well-off people built special tea rooms in their houses, and others, particularly women, had their tea clubs, sometimes using beer halls as their meeting place. "The craze for tea parties finally resulted in the ruin of many homes," one tea authority noted. Women neglected their housewifely duties and the angry men sought solace in the tavern. The custom came in for its share of satire, including the play, *The Tea-Smitten Ladies*, produced in 1701.

After an initial splash, tea never made much headway in France over the traditional beverage, wine, or in Germany over beer. But it became popular in Russia after its arrival by the overland route, making Russia, with Britain, the Old World's other greatest tea drinking nation.

Tea from Tay to Tea

The name for tea is derived not from the standard (Mandarin) Chinese name *cha* but from the same word in the Amoy dialect. The Dutch carried on their earliest China trade from Java, where they met Chinese junks out of the port of Amoy (Xiamen) in Fujian province, just across the strait from Taiwan. Thus they learned the Amoy name *te* (pronounced "tay," but more like "day") and took it to Europe. As all European countries except Russia and Portugal bought their first tea from the Dutch, they too used this name. The Portugese, who traded out of the port of Macao, near Guangzhou, base their word on the Cantonese-derived *cha*.

It is still unclear whether "tay" or "tea" first came to England. In his 1660 diary entry Samuel Pepys wrote "tee," but in 1711, Alexander Pope still rhymed it with "obey" in "The Rape of the Lock," a sound which may have been a fashionable borrowing from the French. In poems from 1712 and 1720 it rhymes indisputably with "knee," indicating that a change must have taken place around that time. The Irish and some others still say "tay."

CARAVANS TO RUSSIA

The first tea reached Russia in 1618, when a Chinese embassy presented some to Czar Alexis. After 1689, when the Treaty of Nerchinsk defined the border between the two, caravan trade began, at China's insistence, through the frontier town Usk Kayakhta (or Kiahta) north of Ulan Bator, then on the Chinese border, today just inside the border of the USSR. Russian government camel trains would arrive laden with furs and return carrying tea. Ordinary caravans of two to three hundred camels took almost a year for the trek from Moscow to the border town and back. The entire journey from Chinese grower to Russian market took eighteen months.

By 1700 Russia was receiving over six hundred camel loads of tea annually, at a cost so great that only aristocrats could afford to buy it. In 1735 Czarina Elizabeth set up a regular private caravan route which made tea more plentiful.

By the death of Catherine the Great in 1796, Russia was consuming over six thousand camel loads of tea per year—something over three-and-a-half million pounds. Regardless of their social or economic status, most Russians ate a single large daily meal and sipped glasses of tea the rest of the time.

Since Chinese ports were not open to Russian ships, the caravan trade continued until 1880 when the first link of the Trans-Siberian Railway was completed. After Guangzhou was opened as a foreign port, Russian entrepreneurs set up mechanized factories there making brick tea, which the Russians favored. In 1882 these were moved to Hankou on the middle Yangtze.

The samovar, a metal water container with a fire underneath and a pipe up the middle which keeps the water hot (to dilute strong tea from a pot on top) probably became widespread in Russia during Czarina Elizabeth's reign. Soon every home in Russia had one as the Russians became avid drinkers of strong tea sipped through a lump of sugar held between the teeth.

Peter Mundy, who chronicled his arrival with the first British ship in Macao in 1637, mentions a Chinese samovar there. The famous tea authority, William Ukers, says the samovar developed out of a Chinese teapot (he pictures one of pewter) that sat atop a brass charcoal burner.

Camel caravans carried tea across Eurasia to Russia.

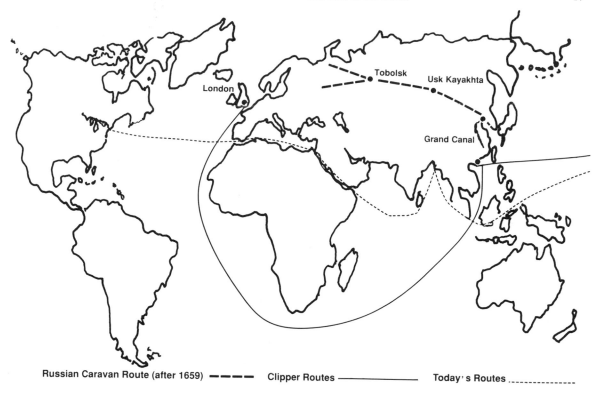

Russian Caravan Route (after 1659) ▬ ▬ ▬ ▬   Clipper Routes ——————   Today's Routes ------------

The charcoal gas escaped through a cone which passed upward through the pot and lid. It bears some relationship to the charcoal-heated firepot for cooking meat in broth still used today by the Mongolians. The samovar is a rarity in China today.

How Tea Traveled.

ALL THE TEA IN ENGLAND

Tea came to England ten years later than to the continent. The first solid evidence of the sale of tea in England is a newspaper advertisement for the coffeehouse of Thomas Garway in London in 1658. It read: "That excellent and by all Physitians approved drink called by the Chineans tcha, by other nations Tay alias Tea is sold at the Sultaness Head a cophee house in Sweetings Rents by the Royal Exchange London." Two years later Garway was to issue a lengthy handbill describing its benefits to health (see p. 163) and stating that while formerly tea had been so scarce as to sell for six to ten pounds sterling per pound of tea, now Garway was selling it for sixteen to fifty shillings.

Coffeehouses had grown up a decade earlier, with the importation of beans from the Middle East. In them men, but not women, of all walks of life could meet for a smoke, companionship, and coffee. At these "penny universities" as they were called (a penny admission) the news of the day was exchanged. The walls were covered with handbills, playbills, and broadsheets, and business and political action were discussed. At one time five hundred such coffeehouses existed in London. They were favorite hangouts and even places of work, where many writers, including Dryden, Pope, and Addison and Steele, gathered information for their early news sheets. Jonathan Swift received letters from his beloved Stella at the St. James coffeehouse. The world famous insurance firm, Lloyds of London, is named for the coffeehouse where it started.

Thomas Twining, who went on to build a great tea business, in 1717 opened the first such house strictly for tea—to women as well as men—and tea began to overtake coffee as the leading non- alcoholic beverage. Secretary of the Admiralty Samuel Pepys recorded in his famous diary having his first cup of tea in 1660, and in 1667 that a druggist recommended it to his wife for her cold.

Eighteenth-century coffee-houses and later teahouses were enlivened by political leaflets and argument.

THE EAST INDIA COMPANY

The East India Company, a group of wealthy merchants, had been chartered by Queen Elizabeth on December 31, 1600, when England, though victor over the warships of the Spanish Armada, lagged far behind in trade. Spain still stood first in the West and Portugal was rivaled only by the Dutch in the East.

It can truly be said that this company helped build the British Empire. Granted a monopoly on all trade east of the Cape of Good Hope and west of Cape Horn, it had rights normally exercised by governments: to acquire territory, coin money, maintain armies and forts, form foreign alliances, declare war, conclude peace, and try and punish lawbreakers. It would hold the greatest monopoly in any commodity that the world has ever known—and that commodity was tea.

Catherine of Braganza, the Portugese bride of England's King Charles II, is credited with popularizing tea in her new home. Daughter of a great trading nation, she had encountered tea early, and Charles had acquired a taste for it while living in exile in Holland after his father, Charles I, had been beheaded by the Protestant revolution led by Oliver Cromwell. Tea came into the public eye when two of Charles' courtiers returned from a mission to Holland with some tea and their wives gave continental-style tea parties, setting a new fashion.

When Charles II came to the throne in the Restoration in 1660 the East India Company, anxious to win the royal couple's favor, presented them with a gift of two pounds of tea—though it was purchased from a coffeehouse. It would be nearly a decade before the company started importing tea directly from the Orient. In 1684 the company succeeded in establishing the first English trading post on China's mainland at Canton. Soon tea made up over 90 percent of China's exports to England. Silk and chinaware or other ceramics came second and third. As tea authorities Joel, David, and Karl Schapira perceptively observe: "Tea was served as much for its strangeness as for its taste. Drinking tea was one way aristocrats of the West could participate in the exciting voyages of discovery being made in their age."

The Chinese emperor decreed that the foreign merchants could dock their ships and trade only at the port of Guangzhou (Canton), and that they had to do business through an appointed Chinese factor. The merchants built a row of two- and three-story "factories" or *hongs* (from *hang* or "business") on a narrow strip of land along the coast. These had warehouses, offices, and living quarters. Ships could remain only through the August-to-March sailing season. Most personnel went to Macao for the rest of the year. The foreign merchants had to pay a certain amount to the emperor based on tonnage of trade, which was collected by the chief official in charge, the hoppo, a term derived from *haiguan bu*, or customs office.

Few people realize how many huge fortunes both in Britain and the

United States were founded on the tiny leaves plucked in the green hills of China. The tea trade was also a respectable occupation for younger sons, and several well-known literary men earned their living in the service of the East India Company, including economists James Mill and his son John Stuart Mill, novelist Thomas Love Peacock, and essayist Charles Lamb.

Milk in Your Tea?

How did the custom of drinking black tea with milk begin? When tea first reached Europe, it was not drunk with milk, although other things including saffron, ginger, nutmeg, and salt were often added. The Dutch, Europe's first tea drinkers from the 1630s on, did not in the beginning use milk. Garway's 1660 London broadsheet, however, declares that it "being prepared with Milk and Water, strengtheneth the inward parts." Yet a 1706 "Poem Upon Tea" by Mr. Tate, poet laureate to Queen Anne, mentions only sugar and not milk.

One theory is that the custom came to Europe through contact with the Mongolians, who today still use milk, or the early Manchus, but there is no proof of this. Chinese sources have so far provided no help on this point, as Chinese today rarely use milk in tea. One exception was recorded by a member of a 1655 Dutch East India Company delegation to the Chinese emperor. Officials who entertained them at dinner in Guangzhou (Canton) served very hot tea boiled down by a third and drunk with one-fourth warm milk and a little salt.

Some think the custom originated in Germany or France. Madame de Sevigny, whose letters published in later years reveal so much about the customs of her time, remarked in 1680 that the idea was invented by Madame de la Sabilere. In fact, in both these countries tea never gained wide popularity. But the custom of milk, carried over to Britain, became a national norm.

TEA BECOMES AN INSTITUTION

In the eighteenth century, tea became an institution, partly with a boost from Queen Anne (r. 1702–14). She started the custom of drinking tea instead of ale for breakfast. She is also credited with originating the use of a large silver teapot instead of the small Chinese ceramic ones. The attraction of tea is described in an oft-quoted passage from Agnes Repplier's 1933 *To Think of Tea!*:

> Tea had come as a deliverer to a land that called for deliverance; a land of beef and ale, of heavy eating and abundant drunkenness; of gray skies and harsh winds; of strong-nerved, stout-purposed, slow-thinking men and women. Above all, a land of sheltered homes and warm firesides—firesides that were waiting—waiting, for the bubbling kettle and the fragrant breath of tea.

Certainly the most famous English verse about the feeling of security a cup of tea evokes must be that by William Cowper, an insecure though reputable poet.

> Now stir the fire, and close the shutters fast,
> Let fall the curtains, wheel the sofa round;
> And while the bubbling and loud hissing urn
> Throws up a steamy column, and the cups,
> That cheer but not inebriate, wait on each,
> So let us welcome peaceful evening in.

England's infatuation with the beverage in the first half of the eighteenth century was so great that it alarmed some observers. An economist complained that money spent on it would better be used for bread, and that teatime wasted hours that should have been spent working. In 1757, Dr. Samuel Johnson gave a thunderous reply to a public letter attacking tea drinking, describing himself as

> A hardened and shameless tea drinker, who has for many years diluted his meals with only the infusion of this fascinating plant;

whose kettle has scarcely time to cool; who with tea amuses the evening, with tea solaces the midnight, and with tea welcomes the morning.

Actually, he might have preferred wine, and is reported to have once downed thirty-six glasses, but realized that with wine he could get no work done. So it was tea that fueled his efforts on the first dictionary of the English language.

The love affair with tea inspired numerous poems about it, and indeed to it. This went on into the late nineteenth century. Tributes to tea appear in the works of Cowper, Thackeray, De Quincey, and even in those of Norway's Ibsen. And the tea party became such an institution that it merited its own literary burlesque in the marvelous Mad Tea Party of Lewis Carroll's *Through the Looking Glass.*

Tea was given a further boost by the temperance movement, which staged mass "tea meetings" promoting it as an alternative to alcoholic gin and ale. But not all crusaders were in the tea camp. The Methodist reformer John Wesley preached against it as a waste of money that could better be spent by the poor on food. (A similar view was held in the United States in the 1830s by Dr. William Alcott, who calculated that an annual expenditure of six dollars per tea drinker added up to $20 million a year, enough to support 50,000 families or employ 50,000 teachers.) What is less widely known about Wesley is that during an illness he turned to tea and became extremely fond of it. Thomas Wedgewood, the porcelain maker, presented him with a huge teapot.

Vauxhall, one of London's popular tea gardens, in 1751.

TEA GARDENS AND SOCIAL LIFE

Soon tea drinking as a way of socializing moved out of the coffee houses and, for the summer at least, into elaborate tea gardens where men and women could meet socially. Greatest and longest-lived was Vauxhall on the Thames near Vauxhall Bridge. Many contained serpentine paths, a bowling green, and a "great room" for concerts and dancing. Tea, as in the teahouses of Song China, was the pretext for socializing. The beverage was served, with bread and butter or small cakes, but promenading and conversing were the major pastimes. Some gardens featured masked carnivals, fireworks, races, gambling, and concerts. Cuper's offered music by Corelli and Handel, the latter being a frequent garden patron, along with Dr. Johnson and novelists Henry Fielding and Horace Walpole.

The vogue passed and gardens proved unprofitable, though Vauxhall endured from its opening in 1732 into the nineteenth century. The last London tea garden closed in the 1850s. But in 1886, a new tea phenomenon appeared, the tea shop. Often these were run by the large tea companies such as Lyons, and served food as well. Tea shops (or shoppes for quaintness) flourished in cottages, too.

By the time the gardens disappeared, tea drinking had moved into the home. The high government tax on imports of tea had made smuggling one of the big businesses of the eighteenth century, but it also brought the price down within the range of non-aristocrats. Many a family purchased its tea from an illicit seller in response to a rap on the window in the night. At one time, so many persons were engaged in smuggling that there was a shortage of farm labor. Unlawful tea was even hidden in church vaults. Various authorities maintain that one-half to two-thirds of Britain's total tea imports entered illicitly.

Adulteration was another industry spawned by the tax, which made the legal price of tea exorbitant. It was done with the leaves of willow, elder, and ash trees, and with used tea leaves. Sawdust, gunpowder, and dried sheep dung were other additives. Forests were ruined and vast tracts were given over to growing leaves just for this purpose. For over a century and a half following the first law against adulteration in 1725, various other tea regulations were passed, but it wasn't until 1875 that legislation finally was successful in halting the practice.

Green tea led over black tea from the start in imports into Britain. But green tea, being unroasted, was easier to adulterate, so people began turning away from it and to the black.

AFTERNOON TEA

In the 1840s Anna, seventh Duchess of Bedford, started afternoon tea in England, and it became an institution. She use to have "a sinking feeling" in late afternoon, having had, as was the custom, little to eat since breakfast and with nothing to look forward to until an eight o'clock dinner. So at five she began taking tea and cakes, and sometimes inviting friends, as had been done earlier in France.

For the benefit of readers of English novels, here is the Schapiras' summary of teatime:

> Gradually, in the eighteenth century, two distinct customs evolved. "Low tea" was aristocratic in origin and consisted of a snack of pastries and sandwiches followed by tea, at around six in the evening. It was a prelude to the really serious eating, which would begin about nine o'clock.
>
> "High tea" or "meat tea" was bourgeois in background, and was made up largely of the leftovers of the huge middle-class lunch: cold meats, relishes, bread, and cheese. These were served with tea to form the evening meal.

The British institution of tea soon extended across all classes, and leaped across the oceans to countries founded by emigration from Britain (although the United States later gave it up). "I'll make you a nice cup o' tea" became the British solution to every problem—or at least served as an excuse to pause while considering further action.

The present-day scene is captured very well in three sentences by Charles and Violet Schafer in their *Teacraft:* "Construction workers shinny down 20 stories twice a day for tea. Shoppers, male and female, dodge into restaurants, snack bars or hotels for theirs. Bobbies on the beat call a halt for tea."

British dockworkers have gone on strike for tea rights. During the times of heavy bombing in World War II, gathering for a cup of tea was a great morale booster, a minute of closeness and a reminder that peace might return. Volunteers in covered vans served it all night and Minister of Labor Ernest Bevin asked employers to provide tea to workers on overtime.

No sheepherder in the Australian outback forgets his tea. In his swag bag or matilda (celebrated in the Australian song about Waltzing Matilda) he carries his wire-handled can, or billy. He boils his water in it, hung over an outdoor blaze if necessary, and then throws in the leaves.

Today the United Kingdom, as the world's largest tea importer, buys a quarter of the tea on the market. Per capita consumption is almost seven pounds a year.

Opium chests being unloaded at a Chinese port.

TEA REPAID WITH OPIUM

Before British tea importing was a century old, by 1769, annual imports reached 4.5 million tons—and paying for the tea was creating a major drain on the crown's currency reserves. China, with plenty of cotton textiles, did not need broadcloth, the main product Britain had available for export earnings. The monetary drain worried even the Swedish botanist Linnaeus, who proposed to "shut the gate through which all the silver was leaving Europe" by growing tea commercially on that continent.

By 1800, the opium trade was providing Britain with the answer to her problem. Opium had long been taken in China, but mainly in Sichuan where it grew. Smoking, introduced with tobacco around 1620, made the drug easy to use. Demand rose and Portugese merchants, followed by British, added to the Chinese stocks. Easy access to opium spurred by its dealers' profit motive caused a runaway spiral of addiction. This poisoning of a nation was rationalized by the claim that it helped the Indian colony generate its own revenue. Indian-grown opium was sold to China for silver, which remained in Canton and was credited against debts in London. Thus, without moving any bullion around, British merchants were able to get silver for opium and then turn and pay for tea with the same silver. The havoc wrought by the rapid growth of addiction aroused the concern of the Qing dynasty government.

China forbade the importation of opium in 1800, on the severest penalties, but the drug kept pouring in illegally, without the import duties the government collected when the trade was legal. Opium was no longer brought to the Canton anchorage, but to an island in the middle of the bay, where it waited on ships till collected by Chinese smugglers, who were allowed in by corrupt Chinese officials bribed by the British.

In June 1839, the official sent to end opium importation, Lin Zexu, burned twenty thousand chests of it on the beach near Canton. Within a year Britain had declared war on China, forcing the nation to legalize the opium trade again. A decade after the end of the Second Opium War of 1857 to 1860, the number of addicts had grown tenfold and imports reached a hundred thousand chests a year. The evil "foreign mud," as it was called, remained a legitimate item of commerce until 1908, and addiction persisted for decades after.

SEARCH FOR THE SECRET

The Chinese tried by every means to keep secret the methods of tea cultivation and processing, as they had earlier the technology of silk production. Imperial edicts prohibited revealing them on the pain of death. False information about tea production was even passed around to confuse outsiders. For three centuries China was successful hiding the mysteries of tea, and was the world's main tea exporter.

Linnaeus was eager to have a tea plant. His student, Per Osbek, transported one to the Cape of Good Hope on a Swedish East India Company vessel, but it was lost in a storm. Another fell into the harbor when the ship's guns fired a departing salute. He did get a plant to Uppsala in Sweden and nourished it with great care—until it was found to be an ordinary camelia. A true tea plant that reached Sweden in 1763 was eaten by rats. Finally a Swedish ship brought some potted seeds, which germinated and grew. But even then, Linnaeus did not know the secret of processing, and assumed that green tea and black tea were two different species.

In 1793 the embassy to China led by Lord Macartney obtained some tea seeds which they took to Calcutta. The next few decades saw several attempts to grow tea outside China from seeds. Dutch growers were successful in Java with both seeds and plants from Japan.

The British East India Company had been uneasy about its total dependence on China for tea long before the Opium War, and from 1788 on had entertained the possibility of growing tea in India. In the early 1830s its Tea Committee circulated a questionnaire to all company employees inquiring about locations with suitable climate and altitude.

In 1823 Major Robert Bruce had actually discovered an indigenous tea used by native people in India's Assam while living with them after the conquest of this remote area. His brother Charles sent specimen branches to the company's botanical gardens at Calcutta, but they were rejected as being another form of the flower camelia. However, when the 1830 questionnaire came round, Charles Bruce replied by sending actual tea seeds, plants, and processed leaves from Assam. The find was declared "the most important and valuable" ever made on agricultural or commercial resources of the Empire.

By this time, China's secret seems to have been out, for the company began importing seeds from China, and the first Assam-grown tea was sold in 1839. In 1848 the company sent the Scottish botanist Robert Fortune to China for plants, expert workmen, and tools. Disguised as a Chinese, he had earlier entered the forbidden interior of China in order to collect plants and seeds. It was Fortune who brought the news that green tea and black tea actually came from the same plant and differed only in processing.

The native strain of Assam tea in fact proved much better in the end. The Chinese plants did not do well in India, and their cultivation was abandoned, but not before they managed to crossbreed with the Indian strain and weaken it.

The Tea Committee probably had no inkling that from these experimental beginnings India would become the world's leading producer of tea. She holds this position today, with output exceeding a billion pounds and a million acres dedicated to tea gardens. Ceylon, formerly a coffee grower, became a producer of high quality tea after the crop was introduced in 1870 as an answer to a coffee blight.

BRITISH AND AMERICANS

Tea figures in two episodes of British-American relations: the American Revolution of 1776 and the rivalry of the clipper ships. Americans drank tea before the British. In l650 Peter Stuyvesant introduced it to the Dutch colony New Amsterdam, and from there it spread throughout North America. A tea meal in Dutch New York is described in Washington Irving's famous short story "The Legend of Sleepy Hollow." Two Bostonians in 1690 became the first English colonists licensed to import tea. One was Zabdiel Boylston, an apothecary, who advertised "green and ordinary" teas at retail.

At first in the English colonies, probably around 1670, the tea leaves were prepared by boiling them a long time, and the bitter liquid was taken without milk or sugar. The flavor obviously could not have excited anyone, so tea's stimulating effect or the belief in its medicinal properties must have been the attraction. Some users also salted the leaves and ate them with butter.

In 1674, when the British took over New Amsterdam from the Dutch and renamed it New York, they found themselves with a colony that probably drank more tea than all England. In imitation of London, coffee houses appeared in New York City, and also tea gardens for outdoor refreshment and socializing. A pump with particularly pure water became the site of one of these gardens at what is now Park Row. There was at least one on the Bowery and another near the intersection of Mulberry and Grand streets. They served tea, coffee, and hot rolls, and in the evening there were fireworks, concerts, and dancing.

Women went to parties, each carrying her own saucer, spoon, and a teacup of the most delicate china that held only as much as a wineglass. All this elegance was cut short by momentous events of history.

The Boston Tea Party: Protestors dumped the contents of three British ships into the harbor.

ALL THE TEA IN BOSTON HARBOR

In 1767, the British Parliament passed the infamous act imposing duties on tea and other commodities imported by the American colonists. The colonists resisted by smuggling in tea from Holland. Although the other duties were repealed in 1770, the one on tea remained, so the colonists continued resorting to this illegal source.

By 1773, the British East India Company, already in financial trouble for internal reasons, had a surplus of 17 million pounds of tea in danger of going stale. So Parliament wrote off the company's debts, gave it a loan, and granted it a monopoly in the colonies through its chosen agents. This drove other American sellers into the legions of disgruntled citizens. The tax of threepence per pound was modest, and added little to Britain's revenues. What rankled was the idea. The tea tax was symbolic of many other grievances, and "taxation without representation" became a rallying cry.

The anger erupted in the Boston Tea Party on December 16, 1773. Too little has been said about the role of the colonial women in the event. The East India Company, now underselling the smugglers, had expected the colonial women to go for their tea. But the insult of being sent stale leaves and taxed for them was the proverbial last straw on top of already high feeling. Pledging to use no tea at home or to boycott it completely, the women held meetings and initiated petitions. Their aim was to prevent the tea from being unloaded so that the duty would not be paid.

The women's action was not confined merely to the Boston area. The women of Edenton, North Carolina, for example, in a declaration published in a London paper, vowed "not to conform to the pernicious

Cartoon by American revolutionary Paul Revere depicts the colonies as a captive maiden forced to drink tea on Britain's taxing terms.

custom of drinking tea, until such time as all Acts which tend to enslave our native country shall be repealed."

On December 16 after a meeting attended by 5,000, fifty men disguised as Indians and armed with hatchets and pistols attacked the three tea ships anchored at Boston. They broke open and dumped into the harbor the East India Company's entire Boston consignment, 342 chests valued at l0,000 pounds sterling. Patriotic anti-tea incidents took place in many parts of the colonies.

By the time the revolution began, most Americans had renounced tea drinking, for a time at least. The tax rankled even after the revolutionary victory. Witness these gloating comments by the poet Philip Freneau for the 1784 departure of the *Empress of China*, the first ship to China from the new United States:

> She now her eager course explores,
> And soon shall greet Chinesian shores,
> From thence their fragrant TEAS to bring
> Without the leave of Britain's king . . .

TWO INVENTIONS

Americans were never again as heavy tea drinkers as Canadians, who did not experience this interruption, although after the revolution George Washington took three cups at breakfast. The United States, however, was the site of the two striking inventions that changed tea style: iced tea and the tea bag.

The first was born at the St. Louis World's Fair in 1904. The tea merchants had set up a colorful Far East House complete with several turbaned Indians to promote Indian black tea. The weather was scorching and nobody was buying the hot beverage. The British Richard Blechynden, who was in charge, in desperation thought of pouring his tea over ice. This was a hit. Iced tea is now drunk by the gallon in the southern United States, and out of the total of 46 billion servings in the nation as a whole, 37 billion are iced. Until that time tea drinkers in the States had clung to their early preference of China green, but black soon outstripped it.

As for the tea bag, in 1908 New York importer Thomas Sullivan sent out samples of his various kinds sewn into little silk bags. Someone mistakenly made an infusion with the leaves still in the bag, and soon Sullivan's customers were complaining when his tea was not in bags. Now half of all tea drunk in the United States is made with tea bags, and the amount used continues to grow.

Today the United States has become the world's second biggest tea importing nation, purchasing a total of 100 million tons from all countries. It is also China's second largest customer, taking 20,000 tons in 1988. U.S. buyers spent $15 million on Chinese tea in 1985. The price averaged $1.20 per kilogram, while the British, who prefer higher grades, paid $1.55 per kilogram. U.S. imports are mostly black tea for use in instant tea and tea bags, but more Americans are now showing an interest in Chinese green and oolong teas.

THE CLIPPER SHIPS

Tea lay behind one of the most colorful eras in U.S. maritime history, the tea trade—the tall, beautiful clipper ships, the intrepid, hard-driving and soon wealthy captains (and the intrepid, hard-driven, far less wealthy seamen), the new fortunes of shipowners and shipbuilders, the high, square New England mansions with widow's walks on top, the exotic curios that were soon displayed in every New England home. These included silks, porcelain, silver dishes, carved ivory, and furniture of carved wood and lacquer, and tens of thousands of fans. Sometimes gifts from seafaring men, and often ship's ballast, as in the case of porcelain, these were an inseparable concomitant of the tea trade. A.B.C. Whipple in *The Clipper Ships* makes the astonishing statement that in 1850 a fifth of every household's goods in Salem, Massachusetts, came from China.

What is less well known about these romantic sailing ships on the

Clipper ships were developed for speedier transportation of tea.

China run is that when tea business was slim, they carried instead to the United States and elsewhere thousands of Chinese laborers fleeing the poverty of their own country by taking the hardest, low-paying jobs abroad.

Tea also promoted a revolution in shipbuilding. Because tea leaves mold in damp sea air, a rapid passage meant a better tea. The long trip from China to the east coast of the United States took six months to a year around Cape Horn, a powerful incentive to design faster ships. The answer was the clipper. Developed out of the swift, maneuverable privateers built to raid British shipping during the War of 1812, it was lean and sleek, with a sharp bow that cut through the waves, and much more sail.

The first true clipper with all of its features was the *Rainbow*, designed by John Willis Griffiths and launched on February 22, 1845. Despite some damage and unfavorable northeast winds, she made the trip in 102 days, sixteen fewer than any vessel previously, and so fast that she was the first to bring back to New York the news of her arrival in Canton. The all-time record for the trip from Canton to Sandy Hook near New York City was made by the *Sea Witch* on March 25, 1849—74 days, 14 hours.

The 1843 Treaty of Nanking at the end of the First Opium War ceded Hongkong to Britain and permitted foreign vessels to enter four more Chinese ports in addition to Canton. Tea shipping became a big business. The British East India Company, though it held on in India until 1859, could no longer claim a monopoly on the tea trade. Many younger companies were challenging it. In 1833 Parliament had repealed the Navigation Acts. Intended to give the British an advantage over the Dutch in shipping, these had specified that only British ships (or Chinese, but there were none so large) could carry Chinese tea to Britain. The repeal provided the opportunity for the faster U.S. ships to enter the British trade. *The Oriental*, the first U.S. vessel to take Chinese tea to London, reached there in December 1850, only ninety-seven days out of Hongkong, far faster than any British ship had ever made the trip.

Without the umbrella of the monopoly, British shipbuilding was forced to create vessels that could compete. Tea had been transported to Britain in the East Indiamen, large, stately craft that moved steadily but slowly—tea wagons they were called. The U.S.-British rivalry in shipbuilding and design aroused as much excitement and apprehension as had the Boston Tea Party, according to some commentators. British shipbuilding rose to the challenge and produced some fine clippers.

The rivalry climaxed in the China-to-London clipper races over the next two decades. The first tea on the London market brought the best price. It became the fashion to offer guests a cup of tea from the newest crop brought by the year's fastest and most famous ship. Spectators crowded to the city, sleeping at the docks. Bets were placed, and the winning crew might divide a bonus of five hundred pounds sterling.

The first Chinese picking would reach one of the treaty ports, usually Fuzhou in Fujian province, in mid-June. The loads were packed with extreme care by skilled Chinese stevedores, for even a slight shift in weight or balance could slow up a ship. In our age of power ships, it is not easy to visualize the difficulties faced on the long trip, with progress subject to the whims of the wind and the waves, and won by pitting the seamen's skill against them. The ships left from Canton or Fuzhou, not knowing, in those days before the telegraph, how their competitors were doing until they neared London.

The greatest race took place in 1866 with an all-British cast of forty vessels. (The best U.S. clippers had either been destroyed in the Civil War or sold by panicky owners to foreign buyers.) Its conclusion, despite 15,000 miles and ninety-nine days, might be described as a photo finish.

The prize was to go to the first ship to toss some tea chests onto the dock. While the *Ariel* waited to take on a pilot at the Dungeness light off the British coast, the *Taeping* came up from behind and passed it. Captain Keay of the *Ariel* moved ahead and cut off the *Taeping*, forcing it to slow down. At the mouth of the Thames River he was leading, but unluckily got a poor tugboat, and the *Taeping* passed him. Still he thought he had won the race, as the *Taeping* had to go further upstream to dock. But low tide kept him from getting alongside his dock. While the *Ariel* waited an hour and twenty-three minutes, the *Taeping* reached its own dock and, able to maneuver better in the deeper water upstream, tied up and tossed its first tea chests over, thus becoming technically the winner.

The last race was in 1871, when steamships had nearly replaced the clippers, and the opening of the Suez Canal had already cut weeks off the sailing voyage from Asia.

Nineteenth-century drawings of tea chests enroute to a river port. Fine teas did not touch the earth: when the carrier rested, the chest was suspended between the poles which were stuck in the ground (left).

THREE 🍃 *Chinese Tea Customs*

The Chinese have no exact teatime like the British, but tea is always offered immediately to a guest in a Chinese home. Serving a cup of tea is more than a matter of mere politeness, it is a symbol of togetherness, a sharing of something enjoyable and a way of showing respect to visitors. To not take at least a sip might be considered rude in some areas. This custom was maintained even through the very hard years, when families offered "white tea," that is, a cup of boiling-hot water.

The hostess will freshen up the cup with more tea from the pot. Some Chinese people used to consider refilling the pot and offering a third cup the signal that it was time to leave, but this custom does not apply among close friends, and many people pay no attention to it today.

In Chaozhou, up the coast from Guangzhou in Guangdong province, and in some other places, people like their tea made in the *gongfu* style (here meaning "brewed with great skill"). The tea set consists of a tiny pot and four handleless cups the size of a walnut half-shell. The best are of Yixing stoneware (see pp. 66–68). The pot is filled half to three-fourths full of tea leaves, and then they are "rinsed" by pouring boiling water over them and immediately draining it off. The pot is then filled about seven-eighths full of boiling water. After one minute the beverage is poured into the cups. The first cup is sipped and savored for its aroma. The second, after the pot has had more water added, is the most flavorful, for by then the infusion has reached full strength. By the third, there is no more aroma, but the flavor is still good. Oolong is particularly suited to this style.

IN A RESTAURANT

At home or in a restaurant the teapot always appears on the table before any meal for the guests to refresh themselves while waiting for the food, and afterward to aid its digestion. Tea is not served with food unless the guest asks for it. In Chinese style this is always green or oolong tea, never taken with milk or sugar.

Sometimes at the end of a seafood course, such as lobster or prawns which diners have had to shell with their fingers, the waiter will bring a basin of hot tea and a few pieces of lemon to be used for washing hands before the next course. Jasmine or some other strong-flavored tea will likely be served to drink at the end of the meal, again to combat the fish odor.

As a rule tea comes with the price of a meal in Chinese restaurants in the United States, and many serve only one kind of tea according to their type of customers. Pu-erh is popular in Cantonese restaurants, and Jasmine with Beijing and Shanghai cuisine. Restaurants serving Western food have black tea.

Chinese teahouses, on the other hand, specializing in tea and serving lighter snack food, tend to offer a wider selection. Cantonese ones may have Pu-erh, Ti Kwan Yin, Shui Hsien, Lung Ching, Show Mee, Jasmine, and Chrysanthemum (not a true tea, but made solely from chrysanthemum flowers), and Pu-erh with Chrysanthemum, commonly called Gookpu.

Public bathhouses are big sellers of tea, as after a hot bath people often lie down to cool off and complete their relaxation with a cup of tea. The hot weather brings out numerous tea stalls. When small private businesses started up again after 1979 in China, these were the first to blossom out along the busy streets.

Privately-run tea stalls outside Qianmen Gate in Beijing.

TEA ON THE JOB

Today, every office desk has its tea mug or glass. Workmates rotate the task of bringing big thermoses of hot water from a boiler elsewhere on the premises, and the first thing office workers do in the morning is to make their tea. Fresh hot water is added to the leaves of green tea throughout the day, and most particularly before a meeting, for almost everyone takes a teacup along.

The farmer who works in the fields in the hot south brings a gourd full of tea from home. He hollows out a bottle gourd and allows it to dry thoroughly. For easier carrying, he may weave a two-handled bamboo basket around it, or he may sling it over his shoulder on a string. In any other container the tea would become as hot as the sun in a few hours. But the gourd keeps the tea cool and preserves its natural flavor. Some field workers keep their gourds in a spring so that they can have an even cooler drink.

Anyone who has traveled in China must wonder how many cups of tea he or she has imbibed by the time the tour ended. Local favorites are served with every stop and at every " brief introduction" at every factory, museum, what-have-you visited, as well as before every meal.

On all Chinese trains, clean, covered mugs are supplied and hot water for tea is brought around by the conductors (they used to bring it in beautiful long-spouted handmade brass kettles). You can buy a pack of green tea for a few *fen*, or use what you have brought along.

TEA AND MARRIAGE

In ancient times when a young woman was about to become engaged— the biggest step in her life—her fiancee's family would present her with a gift of tea, then one of the most precious and expensive things available. Her acceptance of it signaled the matchmaker to stop propos- ing candidates. Today, when a young woman becomes engaged she receives a present which is still called the "tea gift" *(chali)* but is not tea. "Tea gift" has become the term for "engagement."

A related custom of "bride's tea" is followed in several variations in South China and among people of Chinese ancestry in Southeast Asia, the United States, and elsewhere. On the day of the wedding the bride offers a cup of tea to her mother-in-law. By accepting the tea, the elder woman signifies that she accepts the bride as daughter-in-law.

AMONG THE HERDSMEN

For herding peoples, whose traditional diet was meat and milk products, tea has been a necessity for centuries as an aid to digestion and a source of Vitamin C. For the Tibetan herdsman, butter tea is more than just a beverage, it is often a way of eating a meal. Preparing it is one of the daily household chores.

First a piece of brick tea is ground up. Then it is boiled a few minutes in a kettle of water and the leaves are strained off. The liquid is poured into a small tea churn and mixed thoroughly with butter and salt. Then the mixture is transferred to a kettle where it is kept warm, ready to drink at any time. Often a handful of ground *tsamba* (highland barley) is thrown in to make a gruel.

Mongolian milk tea begins the same way, with grinding a piece from a brick of green tea. Then the leaves are either dropped into boiling water or into cool water which is brought to a boil. After the tea has cooked a few minutes at low heat, milk and salt are added. In Xinjiang and Qinghai in the far west the milk is cooked with the tea.

WHO DRINKS WHAT?

China's own people are her best tea customers. Tea drinking rose 30 percent between 1977 and 1987. Yet per capita consumption was estimated in 1988 at only 0.3 kilograms per capita (about half a pound). This is obviously not a measure of average individual consumption because of the great number of children, who are not tea drinkers. Nor is it any indication of cups drunk, because many people use the same leaves all day. And in the city of Guangzhou (Canton) average annual consumption is 1.3 kilograms. Consumption has continued to rise, with green tea still the favorite. China herself consumes nearly 80 percent of her green tea production, but only about 10 percent of her black production.

The most popular teas by area are:

North China	Scented teas
Central China	Green, especially Lung Ching and Pi Lo Chun
South China	Green and oolong
West and Northwest	Pressed or brick tea, green or black

Here is a finer breakdown:

Han nationality (China's majority)	Green, scented oolong, some black in cities
Fujian and Guangdong provinces	Pu-erh, oolong
Hunan province	Green with smoky flavor (Weishan Maojian)
Lower Yangtze valley	Green (Lung Ching, Pi Lo Chun, Mao Feng)
Shanxi and Shaanxi	Hua Juan Cha (Scented curled)
Sichuan	Tuo Cha (Bowl tea, a form of Pu-erh)
Ningxia, Gansu, Qinghai, Xinjiang	Green or dark green brick
Xinjiang and Gansu	Red brick
Tibet	Compressed, cake, wrapped square

FOUR   *The Teahouse, Center of Local Life*

Villages in rural China usually don't have teahouses, but every market or county town has one or more. Historically the teahouse was a center of social life for the men, as it remains in rural areas today. (For women there was the line at the village well.) Peddlers and farmers coming to town with their produce can have a cup, or a bite to eat, and rest and relax in the shade of a woven straw-mat awning.

It is a place to exchange news, meet and talk with friends. Business deals of all kinds are concluded there. In some areas even the phrase *shang chaguanr*, literally "to go to the teahouse," also means to take a dispute to be settled. Teahouses were a favorite hangout for elderly retirees, who might park their pet caged birds on a nail and stay all day, and the teahouse still has this function where there is no village club.

Sichuan province, possibly the birthplace of tea drinking, is famous for its teahouses. But almost as famous are those of the city of Suzhou on the Yangtze, noted for its teahouse ballad singers, and Guangdong province, a great tea producer, known for their evening entertainment of Cantonese songs. An estimated 200,000 people go to Guangzhou's teahouses daily. But teahouses exist in every city and area.

Farmers with towel headgear and retirees with pet birds rest and socialize in a rural teahouse depicted by a peasant painter from Hebei, Jiangsu province.

A FAMOUS PLAY

For China's great novelist and playwright Lao She (1899–1966) the Beijing teahouse was a microcosm of urban life. He chose it for the setting of his 1957 play *Teahouse*, he said, because it was a place where

43

people from all walks of life met. Set in the Yutai Teahouse, which Wang Lifa has taken over from his father in old Beijing, it reflects changes in the lives of some seventy characters through three periods, the Qing dynasty, and the times before and after Liberation in 1949.

At the turn of the century, customers are concerned about the inability of the Qing dynasty to govern and to control the growing foreign influence in China. The Qing dynasty court is busy suppressing the reform movement, which had hoped to save the country. Superintendent Pang, an aging court eunuch, buys himself a wife, the daughter of a desperately poor peasant, with the assistance of Pockmark Liu, a Yutai Teahouse regular. One man who dares to express doubt about the future of the dynasty is arrested.

In the second act, taking place in 1918, the Qing dynasty has been overthrown by the 1911 Revolution led by Sun Yat-sen, but things are no better for the common people as the country is torn between rival warlord factions. In order to keep his business, Proprietor Wang Lifa must constantly pay off the police, army thugs, government spies, and gangsters. The old eunuch is dead, and his widow comes in with his adopted son, who makes a living telling fortunes. Wang's prospects look dim and so do those of the republic.

In 1948, on the eve of the establishment of the People's Republic, Wang, now an old man, has kept his teahouse, but changes in it reflect the times. A larger-than-life poster of U.S. film star Rita Hayworth decorates the wall, and military police of U.S. Army units supporting Chiang Kai-shek call in on patrol. Wang is considering hiring a come-on hostess to keep up with the times and revive his business, which like all trade, is going downhill. He interviews a seventeen-year-old girl brought in by Pockmark Liu, Jr., who maintains his flashy life by pimping.

The play ends on a desolate note, reflecting a country ripe for revolution, as Wang has a last bowl of tea with his elderly cronies, an upright man reduced to selling peanuts and a small industrialist whose factory was declared "traitor property" and confiscated. Then Pockmark Liu, Jr. and the head of the police enter to take over. One plans to add a brothel in the back, the other to use the teahouse to collect information for Communist-hunting.

Considered one of the great dramas of the post-liberation period, the

Poster for the drama **Teahouse.**

play has had two successful revivals, a film version, and has been performed in several Western European countries.

Recently a real old-style teahouse with drum singers and other folk artists opened in Beijing, appropriately called the Lao She Teahouse. Places of this kind were closed down during the Cultural Revolution (1966–1976), wrote the well-known writer Deng Youmei, who said he could not see what they threatened. He described the old teahouses as a place where people with very little money could still enjoy entertainment, and hailed the new one as an auspicious sign "first and foremost of people's sense of culture."

Today's teahouses are quite different from Lao She's. They are places of conviviality and quiet bustle. Unsavory characters, should they crop up, are no longer dominant. There are a lot more teahouses in the rural areas now, as they are one of the easier small private enterprises to start up under the new economic policy. The gambling, which was also available in a corner of the old teahouses, still exists, but it is among friends, not organized as a business venture, and kept within bounds. Each locality has its own viewpoint on such forms of recreation.

Localities have their own teahouse customs, too. In Canton one hits the knuckles or fingertips on the table to signify thanks after receiving more hot tea. Many people do this, but few know the story behind it. Once Qing dynasty Emperor Qian Long (r. 1735–1796) made an incognito tour of South China, taking with him only one manservant, named Zhou Riqing. When they ate at teahouses and inns, of course the servant served the master. But sometimes Qian Long, filling the teacups, would pour for his servant too. Zhou felt embarrassed at such honor, but could not reveal his master's identity by kneeling and kowtowing in public to thank him. Finally he invented a way to express his thanks—hitting his knuckles on the table to represent a kowtow. Since then it has become a gesture of thanks throughout South China.

If one wants more hot water, the cover of the teapot is left ajar to catch the waiter's eye. When the guests are finished and the bill is paid, the waiter himself will leave the cover ajar to signify that the table can be cleared. About this there is also a story. A poor man ate in a restaurant without money to pay. When the waiter came around he claimed that he had put his pet bird into the pot for safekeeping and the waiter had removed the lid and let it out. He created such a scene that the

A quiet moment in a Sichuan
teahouse.

A quiet moment in a Sichuan teahouse.

proprietor allowed him to leave without paying, and ever since then, waiters have left covers halfway on, so that any birds inside cannot escape.

Sizable teahouses exist in most large city parks. On weekdays, elderly chess players may be prominent among the customers. But on Sundays they are outnumbered by families, from grandmothers to babes, on holiday outings.

The teahouse still provides a place to cinch a business deal or a setting for friends hatching ideas for further small businesses. Very recently a new figure, the business broker, has reappeared. In an economic situation where business is expanding faster than channels of information about raw materials and markets, brokers supply this information, and even commodities, meeting their clients in the teahouses.

Everyone in Chongqing, capital of Sichuan, a province famous for its teahouses, knows in exactly which one to find brokers for each branch of industry and commerce. Brokers and their clients make up over half of some establishments' regular daytime customers. They are easily identifiable by their almost *de rigueur* dark gray suits (worn unbuttoned) and black briefcases. While there have been some cases of fraud, under the present economic policy the brokers are serving a purpose—and the teahouse is adapting itself to changing Chinese life.

In a Sichuan Teahouse

A TRADITIONAL PORTRAIT BY FAN SUI

I t was a typical Sichuan rural teahouse. High on the wall opposite the door hung a black horizontal tablet whose large raised gilt characters read: "Hujia Teahouse." Beneath the tablet was a brick platform for performances. The other walls were covered with traditional landscape paintings and New Year pictures. The furnishings were comfortable though simple, consisting chiefly of bamboo chairs and square tables, some of which were strewn with books, newspapers and chessmen. Through a side door I could see a small garden with flowers and clumps of bamboo.

It happened to be market day and the place was doing a brisk business. As the tea was served in local style—brewed directly in the bowl-like covered cups—the white-clad attendants were busy moving from table to table with their shiny long-spouted copper kettles, filling the cups with boiling water. Customers had a choice of three types of tea—Jasmine, Chrysanthemum, and *Tuo Cha*, a high-grade of leaf steamed and pressed into cakes in the bottom of a bowl. The price per cup was four or five *fen*, with no extra charge for refills of water.

I was impressed by the way a young waiter, kettle in one hand and his other balancing a pile of six or seven cups with lids and saucers, shuttled adroitly among the crowded tables with great ease. When pouring, he kept the spout at just the right height so that not a drop of water was spilled and the leaves in the cup turned over the proper number of times. He knew just how much water to put in so that the tea would be the right strength. Experience is required to make every cup of tea look attractive, smell inviting, and taste fresh—even a refill where the leaves have already been brewed once or twice. That, said Manager Li, is the real test of the attendant's skill.

Conversation in the teahouses is a popular way of passing the time in Sichuan, so such establishments are found in even the most re-mote places. Most of them, like this one, are run by the supply and marketing co-ops. Others are managed by parks, cultural halls, chess societies and storytelling troupes. In Hujia, with a population of 2,000, there are four of them, all flourishing.

Manager Li, who had been a waiter there before the liberation, said

Teahouse in the open air.
Drawing by Wu Guanzhong

that then the sale was two hundred cups a day, but now four to five hundred is considered an average day's business. Listening to him, I was able to visualize how the place must have looked in the past. The clientele consisted of idlers without any definite occupation, travelers, itinerant herb doctors and peddlers, pot-bellied merchants, and once in a while a working man who came seeking a sympathetic ear into which to pour his misery. The most regular customers were the swaggering landlords, usurers, and local bigshots, and the thugs they employed. They came to gamble, to collect their debts, and trade in women.

The teahouse was also the place where local news made the rounds. Here one learned that the son of the Li family had been pressganged into the Kuomintang army, that the Zhang family's land was going to be taken from them to pay some debt. When such a thing happened, the town's "prominent citizens" would be called upon to "mediate" and the site of the meeting was invariably the teahouse. Of course a poor man could gain nothing in such "mediation." The Li family would have to scrape together a large bribe for the village officials in order to redeem their son; the Zhang family would have to pay their debt eventually, even if they had to sell some children to do it. . . . And on top of it pay for the tea drunk at the "negotiation."

The Hujia Teahouse opens early in the day to please the connoisseurs, who maintain that the morning air gives the tea a particularly refreshing taste. Three cups of a good brew make the spirits soar, they say. Older people with coughs are also among the early customers.

(From *China Reconstructs*, April 1964)

Painting from the early days of the republic (after 1911) pictures a teahouse like that in the Lao She play.

FIVE 🍃 *The Japanese Art of Tea*

T ea drinking for spiritual refreshment reaches its ultimate in the *cha-no-yu*, the tea ceremony for which Japan is famous. The *cha-no-yu* (meaning "hot water for tea," so named to sound more impressive than just plain *cha*) is far more than a ceremony, or even a custom. More suitable is the term Way of Tea—a way of looking at things, an art of living intimately linked with artistic appreciation. In it are echoes of the early history of tea drinking in China, which developed into something uniquely Japanese when transplanted to the islands.

The tea ceremony, even in its simpler form, is more than an elaborate ritual. It is an interlude in which one lends oneself for the moment to the spirit of beauty, quietude, and politeness toward others. The ceremony may be practiced anywhere, at home or in a teahouse.

Here is how it might take place in a large house which has a separate tearoom, actually a rustic tea hut, as has been the form since the late sixteenth century. (Note that this description covers only the main points of the ceremony, not all of the actions or those of any particular school.) Guests, no more than five, assemble in an arbor in the garden in preparation for entering the tearoom. In some schools of the tea ceremony, each will take out a small folded fan about five inches long and tuck it into his or her belt. It symbolizes the swords once used by the samurai warriors, and placing it correctly on the floor is an important part of the later ceremony.

Then the guests proceed down the "dewy path" of stepping stones. This passage through the quiet garden signifies breaking ties with the workaday world outside. The guests may be met at a central gate by the bowing hostess (more often than host these days) and wordlessly led into the inner garden. Or, they may not be greeted until she enters after they are seated.

At a stream of water trickling musically from a bamboo spout into a basin hollowed out of stone, built low to create an attitude of humility, the guests wash their hands and rinse their mouths. "The sound of tinkling water splashing into the stone basin washes the dust from your mind," wrote the sixteenth century tea master Rikkyu. Nearby stands an artistic low stone lantern to light the path for evening. These two often come in fanciful shapes. The origin of the latter is believed to be a pagoda-shaped incense burner used in Korea.

The tea hut stands about two feet above the ground. Leaving their shoes behind, guests enter on their knees through a low, nearly square door—again humility—which puts everyone on the same level. Beside the door hangs a decorative broom often used to clean the path of all but a few artistically-strewn leaves.

The room inside is rarely larger than four and a half tatami mats, or about ten feet square. This is the size of a room in which, according to a Buddhist sutra from India, King Vikramadytia greeted the bodhisattva

Guests in a traditional Japanese garden pass from the arbor (left) along the path past the stone lantern to the teahouse (right). Old Japanese drawing shows guests entering the low door.

Manjushiri and eighty-four thousand disciples, a tale implying that for the truly enlightened, space does not exist. The original characters for this room's Japanese name have been translated to mean "abode of fancy."

The room is completely plain, but beautifully crafted of seasoned wood, with paper windows. Yet it will not be without its variety. No design repeats itself, no two of the tea things will be the same shape. In a shallow alcove hangs a scroll with a verse and occasionally an ink drawing. The calligraphy is changed to fit the "theme" of the season or that day's ceremony. Placed below it or hanging on the wall is a vase with a single flower.

One can lose oneself for as long as four hours in the ceremony; its movements of bowing and handling the tea things follow a prescribed pattern. On their knees and bowing from the waist, the guests note with appreciation the beauty of the scroll, the flower, and the finely crafted iron teakettle bubbling over a charcoal fire recessed in the floor. Then they sit back on their heels in appropriate places around the sides of the room.

According to some styles, the hostess will not enter until all the guests have been seated, and then brings in the tea things one by one. Such a service is described in *The Book of Tea* by one of the earliest modern commentators on the ceremony, Okakura Kakuzo.

> Quiet reigns with nothing to break the silence save the note of the boiling water in the iron kettle. The kettle sings well, for pieces of iron are so arranged in the bottom as to produce a peculiar melody in which one may hear the echoes of a cataract muffled by clouds, of a distant sea breaking among the rocks, a rainstorm sweeping through a bamboo forest, or of the soughing of pines on some faraway hill.

First comes a "moist sweet," often of a gelatinous nature, and then a dry one, both eaten with a pick piece by piece out of a paper napkin. Meanwhile the hostess rinses the drinking bowls with hot water and pours the used water into a special jar. She wipes each bowl with a cloth napkin three times.

The hostess puts the bright green powdered tea, *matcha*, into the first bowl with a long, thin scoop carved from bamboo, using a measure and a half. Then, adding enough water for three and a half mouthfuls, she whips the contents of the bowl to a beautiful light green froth with a tiny bamboo whisk, as was done in Song dynasty China. The principal guest takes the bowl, saying, "Excuse me for drinking before you," and acknowledging the hostess's efforts with the words, "I gratefully accept the tea you have prepared."

The tea finished, the drinker wipes the bowl with a paper napkin and turns it upside down to further examine its design and the mark of the craftsman, if it bears one, and the ceremony proceeds through all the guests. Then the tea caddy and other utensils are appreciated. "What kind of caddy is this?" asks the principal guest, along with other questions about origin and craftsmanship. Finally, the hostess removes the utensils and exchanges bows with each of the guests as they leave.

Of all the authorities consulted in preparing this chapter, no one has described the spirit of the Japanese tea ceremony more beautifully than Professor Michiko Hiramatsu, director of the Japanese Cultural Center at Foothill College in Los Altos Hills south of San Francisco. Here is her explanation intact.

Harmony, one of the Four Principles, also means harmony with nature.

There are four principles: harmony, respect or reverence, purity, and tranquility (*wa, kae, sae, jubuo*).

Harmony means with other people and with nature. The vapor from the boiling water is like floating clouds, the sound of the water like the wind passing through pines. The tea ceremony is the Way of bringing one's self into harmony with nature. Capturing this moment is one aim of the ceremony. The simple result of drinking the tea is to satisfy thirst, but it also satisfies the thirst for knowledge, truth, and tranquility. This is the tea ceremony in its broadest sense.

Respect means a harmonious relationship with others. It includes a kind of selflessness. The stones along the path are to tread upon. They serve the person. The water too is selfless. By using itself it takes away dirt. The stone lantern consumes itself to light the way. We pass through the low door to remind ourselves how humble everyone is.

We each wash our hands and rinse our mouths. This is to remind ourselves of inner cleanliness, to first purify the inner self. We leave other thoughts outside, so our minds are spotless.

We cleanse ourselves through the five senses. Upon entering, the sound of the water, the clink of the dipper, remind us of the silence outside, and our sense of hearing is cleansed. We view the flowers and our sight is cleansed. We touch the utensils, the transformation of mere clay into objects of beauty, and our sense of touch is cleansed. The scent of the flowers and the incense cleanse our sense of smell, and the tea cleanses our sense of taste. When all the five senses are cleansed, the inner self is also cleansed.

Tranquility is the most important. It means living with other people and respecting others. Then you feel tranquility and peace of mind. You accept who you are. You may not be clever or beautiful, but you are uniquely you. This is the true sense of tranquility.

Tranquility also means using something that to you is beautiful, like a handmade basin of bamboo. Finding beauty in nature's abundance, this, too, is tranquility.

HOW THE CEREMONY DEVELOPED

The way the tea ceremony grew up is a fascinating history of back-and-forth relations between Japan and China and then of Japan's innovations.

Tea was introduced from China in the seventh century, but soon afterward Japan's relations with China took a turn for the worse and through the tenth and eleventh centuries almost all contact ceased. Things Chinese, including tea, fell out of favor with the court. Surviving, however, was the custom of monks drinking tea from a single bronze bowl before a statue of Zen Buddhism founder Bodhidharma. To participate in the ceremony is to pray that through drinking the tea, the Buddha and the self will become one, and at the same time offering the self to the Buddha.

Tea was reintroduced into Japan by the monk Eisai, first to visit China after normal relations were resumed. Returning in 1191, he brought two important things—more tea seeds, and the teachings of the Rinzai sect of Zen Buddhism. From China's Song dynasty capital, Eisai brought its new powdered green tea.

Rinzai Zen spread and so did its tea ritual. This was a time when ritual and regulation had become very important. The values of the militaristic set had much in common with the self-discipline, austerity, and idea of defiance of death of Rinzai Zen, and the two reinforced each other. Because the lives of the monks in the Zen sects were so regulated, their tea practice developed greater aspects of ceremony.

Eisai was strong on tea's medicinal value and wrote Japan's first tea book, *Notes on the Curative Effects of Tea*, and also a work on the ceremony for drinking powdered tea. His time coincided with the rise of the samurai warrior families who were taking over power from the declin-

ing royalty. When Sanemoto, one of the military dictators, felt ill after heavy drinking, he called in Eisai and asked that he cast some spells to cure him. Eisai instead prescribed tea. The cure worked, and Sanemoto became a promoter for tea. Its drinking spread beyond the temple and into samurai circles.

Over the next century the big families began holding tea-tasting contests (by the thirteenth century over a hundred varieties existed in Japan) just as Chinese officials had earlier. Despite austere Zen precepts, these became quite lavish at times. The interior elements of alcoves, flower arrangements, and hanging scrolls of Chinese landscape paintings which are part of tea architecture today can be said to date from that time.

In the beginning, utensils used in tea service were imported from China. They included bronze flower containers and vessels for water to wash the bowls, iron teakettles, ceramic tea caddies, and celadon or white porcelain bowls. In the mid-1300s the shoguns started collecting these as art objects and displayed them ostentatiously. They became increasingly valuable, and much of the etiquette in the tea ceremony developed out of delicate ways to handle them. This trend was to change within a few centuries as a new viewpoint developed which was to have a lasting effect on Japanese art.

This new view, *wabi*, has been variously defined as quiet simplicity, finding satisfaction in poverty, love of solitude. It emphasized the artistic value of unadorned, natural, and even unattractive objects. Following traditional Buddhist ideas, imperfect objects, whether natural or crafted, and those lacking ornamentation, evoke deeper, more spiritual feelings. This view recognizes the intrinsically beautiful characteristics in imperfection, thus giving the viewer a more active role in appreciating that beauty, and thereby creating a more spiritual experience.

The roots of *wabi* lie in the love of the simple, solitary, hermit-like life that is part of Buddhism and also Taoism, another religious influence in Japan. The *wabi* view began to surface in the utterances of the monk Murata Shuko (or Juko, 1521–1591). Shuko was threatened with expulsion from the temple for continually falling asleep during daytime meditation, so the story goes. He went to a doctor, who prescribed tea.

Shuko grew so fond of it that he served it to everybody with considerable ceremony.

The shogun Yoshimasa heard about it and invited Shuko to create a tea ceremony for him. Shuko thus became known as the first tea master and founder of the tea ceremony, though Japanese authorities cannot agree as to whether a kind of secular tea ceremony existed before him. In Shuko's time tea drinking became so popular among the common people that tea stands appeared along the highways.

Tea drinking among the samurai was often accompanied by viewing of the full moon from a second-story balcony of a garden tea pavilion. To Shuko is attributed the comment, "I have no taste for the full moon." This is taken variously to mean a criticism of the lavish tea gatherings, and indirectly of the almost total use of Chinese tea things, for Shuko is also quoted on the beauty of Japanese ones. Another meaning of the quote is that he preferred the asymmetrical beauty of a moon partly covered by clouds, or what has been called "the worship of the imperfect."

Shuko replaced Chinese landscape paintings with calligraphy of Zen mottoes. He also believed that the proper quiet could not be achieved in a room in a larger building and that tea should be served in a small hut, but it remained for his pupil Soju to realize this ideal.

Another big step in this direction was taken by Jo-o (1502–1555), an

Tranquility.

official of the lower ranks, after he became a tea master. He maintained that peace of mind could never be attained in the tearoom of his day, which was a reception room in a larger building. He built an isolated tea hut like a peasant home, and used vessels of common Japanese-made pottery. He is considered originator of the *wabi* tea ceremony.

THE STORY OF SEN NO RIKKYU

Sen no Rikkyu (1521–1591), pupil of Jo-o, is a giant among tea masters. A story about the two illustrates *wabi*. Jo-o had swept his garden very clean and asked Rikkyu what he thought of it. The latter shook a few leaves off a tree to give the garden the perfect touch it needed.

Rikkyu became tea master for the military dictator Totomi Hideyoshi, who, having united the warring provinces, wanted to use tea to reconcile their differences. Though a militarist, Hideyoshi understood tea and wanted to use it to pacify the people and resolve differences after the civil war. He asked Rikkyu to reform the ceremony, and thus it was stabilized. The four principles described above by Professor Hiramatsu (harmony, respect, purity, tranquility) stand as formulated by him. His list of rules includes not only ritual but the philosophy of tea.

While the triumphant Hideyoshi built a tearoom with walls covered with gold leaf and served in vessels of gold, Rikkyu moved further and further in the direction of *wabi*. It was he who, impressed by a small passageway on a boat traveling between two islands, gave the tea hut its low door. He took delight in a fisherman's creel and used it as a flower vase. He created a vase of ordinary bamboo, with a natural crack that made it for him all the more artistic. The elegantly simple Tai-an teahouse believed to have been built by him in 1582 still stands inside the Myoki Temple near Kyoto.

Bowls of raku ware, the most famous of all Japanese teaware, were created under his influence. Of porous pottery with a thick glaze in black or red, they are not thrown on a wheel but are manually shaped with slight irregularities to fit the hand and lips, and to evoke the spirit of *wabi*. The first of them were made by the potter Chojiro under Rikkyu's guidance. The name *raku*, meaning "enjoyment or contentment," comes from a seal given by Hideyoshi to Chojiro's brother, the first of a long line of potters to continue his work.

The rift between Hideyoshi and Rikkyu continued to widen until Hideyoshi condemned the master to death in his seventy-first year. One version of the story is that Rikkyu would not allow the dictator to marry his daughter. Another is that Hideyoshi feared that Rikkyu was becoming more influential than he himself. Rikkyu's enemies, playing on these fears, told the dictator that the master was planning to put poison in his tea.

At least Rikkyu was given the honor of taking his own life. Inviting his dearest pupils to his tearoom, he made tea for the last time and then gave each of them a tea implement. The last cup, polluted, he said, by his misfortune, he broke, so that no one else could use it. Then he removed his tea robe, under which he wore the white robe of death, and slashed his abdomen with a sword.

The tea ceremony and the meaning with which Rikkyu had imbued it was carried on by his sons and pupils after his death. It was widely taken up, perhaps as an escape from feudal regimentation, perhaps as a kind of eternal truth to cling to in a period of incessant wars. By the fifteenth century it was fully established among the populace as a whole, and several schools had grown up. The sense of *wabi* that the early tea masters helped to develop is what has made Japanese art different from any other, down to today.

Writing in 1906, Okakura Kakuzo explained why historically the tea ceremony gained popularity in the centuries after Rikkyu's death:

> It is in the Japanese tea ceremony that we see the culmination of tea ideals. Our successful resistance of the Mongol invasion in 1281 had enabled us to carry on the Song movement so disastrously cut off in China itself through the nomadic inroad. Tea with us became more than an idealization of the form of drinking; it is a religion of the art of life. The beverage grew to be an excuse for the worship of purity and refinement, a sacred function. . . . The tearoom was an oasis in the dreary waste of existence where weary travelers could meet to drink from the common spring of art appreciation. The ceremony was an improvised drama whose plot was woven about the tea, the flowers, and the paintings. Not a color to disturb the tone of the

room, not a sound to mar the rhythm of things, not a gesture to obtrude on the harmony, not a word to break the unity of the surroundings, all movements to be performed simply and naturally, such were the aims of the tea ceremony.

As Japan modernized in the nineteenth century, the tea ceremony was in danger of extinction. Women were a main force giving it new life, and now they are the majority of the tea masters, carrying on the tradition and teaching it as an example of polite conduct and human relations.

A dozen major schools exist in Japan today. About half of them are practiced in many cities across the United States, often for public participation. The Japanese Cultural Center at Foothill College has a small but exquisite garden and an authentic tearoom designed by a Japanese architect. Classes are given at the college, in a park in the nearby town of Saratoga, and elsewhere (the Urasenke school of the tea ceremony founded by Sotan-Urasenke societies exists in San Francisco, New York, and some other cities).

Guests drinking tea.

Of course the ceremony is only for special occasions, but tea (loose green *sencha*) is widely drunk as a beverage all through Japan. A Japanese source claims its per capita use is twice that of China. There is also considerable interest in tea's role in health. Japan and China are the countries that have done the most research on this topic.

SIX 🍃 *Ceramics and Other Tea "Equipage"*

Ceramics must predate tea in Chinese history, but regardless of which came first, the two have gone hand in hand. The least we can say is that Shen Nong, when the leaves of the tea plant fell into his pot, could have been boiling his water in a tripod pottery vessel with three hollow legs to hold it over the fire. (An early history book says that Shen Nong "cultivated plants and made pottery." The use of metal was not to come along until a thousand or so years later.)

As tea drinking came into fashion in the Tang dynasty, it demanded the proper artistic utensils—bowls of fine porcelain, which were a pleasure to handle as well as use, and later, teapots and tea sets. It provided a stimulus to ceramics production in both China and the West. In China, styles in tea drinking also influenced the shape of tea ceramics.

Little is known about utensils used for tea in its early days. We hear about such things in detail only after tea drinking became an art in the Tang dynasty. Ceramics had taken a big leap in the sixteenth century B.C. from pottery to proto-celadon of fine-textured clay with a thick blue-green glaze. It made another leap between the third and fifth centuries A.D. with the appearance of true porcelain, fired at a much higher temperature so that it was thin, translucent, and hard enough to give a clear ring when struck. Both were used for tea bowls when the beverage came into its own in the Tang times.

LU YU'S TEA THINGS

Tang tea came in bricks. A chunk was cut off, roasted, rolled to break up the lump, and boiled in water. In his tea classic, Lu Yu describes a wide-mouthed iron cauldron used for boiling, but says silver is better for long wear. Salt, orange peel, onions, dogwood berries, or peppermint were boiled with the leaves or tossed in later. The brew was sipped from wide bowls. Lu Yu's tea was a complex operation involving altogether twenty-seven pieces of equipment including brazier and fire tools, various containers, scoop, roller, ladle, bowls, and basket for a set for ten. In case the host wanted an outdoors tea-and-poetry-writing excursion at a distant place, there was even a carryall into which could be fitted all the equipment, or "equipage" as it became known in another part of the world, England, in another century.

Although Chinese ceramic pieces had handles since very early times, handleless bowls continued to be favored for tea. An inventive woman of the Tang dynasty, who is known only as the daughter of the military official Cui Ning, made a major contribution to tea equipment—the saucer—sometime between 674 and 680. According to legend she regularly made tea for her father, but found it difficult to hand him the hot bowl. First she tried putting an iron plate underneath, but the bowl slipped around. Then she used a blob of wax to hold it, but that was unaesthetic. She finally asked a lacquer craftsman to make her a small plate with a circular ridge in the center to hold the cup, and the saucer was born. Cups and saucers came in sets from the Song dynasty on, but most bowls continued to be used without saucers until the Ming dynasty.

Wide, shallow stoneware tea bowl, Song dynasty.

THE AESTHETICS OF TEA BOWLS

With tea now an art, its aesthetic appearance in the bowl assumed new importance. Lu Yu wrote that the best tea bowls were from Yuezhou (now Shaoxing in Zhejiang province). Their blue-green color intensified the green of the tea, and white porcelain from Xingzhou (now Xingtai in Hebei province) did the same for tea with a reddish cast.

Yellow bowls from Shouzhou (in Anhui) gave reddish tea a rust tone, and brown ones from Hongzhou made such tea look black. These last were unworthy of tea, he said.

Yuezhou was one of the places famed for bluish-green *yue* celadon, which was likened to jade. (The name is not Chinese but French, from the color of ribbons worn by the shepherd boy Celadon in the play *L'Astree*, produced in 1610, just when this Chinese porcelain reached Europe.) This "secret color" *(mi se)*, as it was known in Chinese, was celebrated by Xu Xin, a poet of the time, in a verse, "The Secret-Color Porcelain Teacup Left Behind from the Tribute."

> Blend green and blue into a refreshing hue,
> We offer new porcelain as tribute to the throne;
> The cups cleverly fashioned like the full moon softened by
>   spring water,
> Light as thin ice, setting off the green tea
> Like an ancient mirror and dappled moss on a table,
> Like dewy budding lotus blooms bidding the lake farewell,
> Green as the fresh brew of Zhongshan's bamboo leaves.
> How can I drink my fill, ill and frail as I am?

Celadon and white were the two main schools of porcelain in Tang. An excellent all-black porcelain was also produced. Two of the most famous Tang ceramics were not used for tea. One was pottery with a three-color glaze in yellow, green, and cream. Statuary and vessels of it became a status symbol in burials, its widest use. Red glaze made with copper, begun in Tang, reached its height in Song. A further development was produced through firing a galaxy of shades, red suffused with purple for example, on a single piece. This became known as *jun* porcelain for the old name of its birthplace, Junzhou (now Shenzhou, in Henan province).

In the Song dynasty powdered tea came into fashion. A lump cut from a brick was ground to a powder and mixed with hot water in a bowl. It was whipped to a froth with a small bamboo brush-like whisk and after a few moments, when the powder had settled to the bottom, the liquid

Yixing red clay pot in narcissus shape, seventeenth-eighteenth century.

was drunk from the bowl. Bowls became deeper and also wider at the top to facilitate whipping. The Japanese still use the whipping method in their tea ceremony. The powdered tea is a beautiful, live green, and the whipped beverage is a lovely color several shades lighter. It is easy to see why tea was called "the river of jade" at that time. The best kind of tea, according to the "Tea Emperor" Song Hui Zong, turned white when whipped. Dark-colored bowls were preferred to create a contrast, particularly those of dark blue, almost black, porcelain. A favorite was black with white lines in the glaze known as "rabbit's fur" made in Fu county, Fujian.

FROM WINE POT TO TEAPOT

The change from powdered to leaf tea, and from whipping to steeping, necessitated a vessel to steep the tea in, and finally the teapot was born. Teapot-type vessels with spout and handle had existed in China since Neolithic times. Some of these ewers are most beautiful and fanciful, shaped like animals or with spouts in shapes like a chicken's head. They were used for water or wine. Tea boiled in a cauldron or whipped in a bowl did not need a teapot. When the custom of infusing the leaves took over, the ewer shape was adapted for tea.

There had been a few earlier teapots—one of famous Tang red *jun* glaze and a Song-Yuan eight-lobed celadon pot, to name two cited by ceramics commentators. But even if evidence shows that these were used for tea, it is unlikely that they were made for that beverage. This is the opinion of K. S. Lo, who has made a study of the famous teapots produced in the town of Yixing in Jiangsu province. Lo believes that the first pots made especially for tea appeared around 1500 and were copies of wine pots long produced at Yixing. As the earliest mention of them, he cites a book of the late Yuan dynasty (that is, before 1368) wherein a man buys a teapot.

Yixing had made fine pottery vessels since 2500 B.C. A monk at a temple nearby is credited with creating the first teapot of Yixing "purple sand" *(zisha)* unglazed stoneware in the early 1500s and "the true form of the Yixing teapot" began thereafter with the potter Gong Chun, called the father of the Yixing teapot. A six-lobe pot bearing his name and the date 1513 is treasured today. As more tea was steeped in pots, it was noted that stoneware kept it warmer than porcelain, and Yixing pots gained wide popularity. Yixing also adjusts better to changes in temperature, and is easier to make because it is fired at 500 degrees lower heat.

The monks saw the advantages of Yixing teapots and spread the word. The pots were soon taken up particularly by the officials and literati. This was probably a gesture to set themselves apart from the court, which used fine porcelain, and the vulgar rich, who displayed their wealth in gold and silver pots. With starkly simple lines that brought out the beauty of the material, or with a minimum of tasteful decoration, the pots made a statement on what their users regarded as the spirit of tea.

Yixing pots were also created in many ingenious shapes—a bamboo trunk, a fruit known as Buddha's Hand, flowers (the six-lobe type represents a lotus). Some were decorated with verses in fine calligraphy. All were molded by hand. A scholar frequently would have a teapot made to order, with whatever artistic conceit he fancied. Many were tiny pots for individual use and the owner drank from the spout.

In addition to their beauty, Yixing pots are prized by tea connoisseurs

TEA AND CERAMIC STYLES

Dynasty	Kind of Tea	Shape	Color
Tang	Boiled	Wide bowl (*zhan*)	Celadon, white with additives
Song	Powdered green, whipped	Deep, wide	Black, deep colors
Yuan		Continuation of Song, as far as is known	
Ming	Loose, infused	Teapot invented, no-handle cup	Yixing, blue and white
Qing	Loose, infused	Covered cup (*zhong*)	Multicolor designs

Yixing pot.

for their affinity for the beverage. A seasoned pot acquires a flavor of its own which contributes to the enjoyment. Yixing ware is made of various local sandy clays which on firing can be made to turn reddish brown, buff, or green. As time went on, Yixing teapots were exported in great numbers to Japan and the West.

MING/QING — CUPS, BRIGHTER COLORS

In the Ming dynasty, with tea infused in pots, wide bowls were replaced by smaller, more delicate handleless cups rarely larger than a Western cup. Wider bowls were believed to dissipate the fragrance of the beverage. The smaller cups often came in sets of four or more with a teapot, all on a round tray bearing the same design.

Also popular for preparing an individual drink of tea was the *zhong*, a saucer and bowl with a lid, to keep the aroma from escaping, invented in the Qing dynasty. The saucer, balancing the bowl, is held in the left hand, while the right hand clamps on the lid, which is just slightly ajar. As one sips the tea, the lid keeps back the leaves. Today, people simply pour their brew into another cup while holding the tea leaves inside the *zhong* bowl with the lid.

Most prized of all tea things were those of porcelain from Jingdezhen in northeastern Jiangxi province. They achieved such a vogue that the court ordered new sets almost daily, and ministers risked death to suggest a curb on such extravagance. The area had produced ceramics since the first century A.D. Nearby is Gaoling, the village that has given its name to kaolin, the fine white clay needed in porcelain production, so Jingdezhen became famed for its porcelain. The white tea bowls popular in the Tang came from there. By Song times the area was a national porcelain center. The area received its present name, meaning Jingde Town, after the Song court ordered sets of porcelain stamped with the characters for the Jingde reign (1004–1007).

New technology brought new beauty—Ming blue and white cups, tea sets, and porcelain of all kinds were to start a vogue in both China and Europe. This was the result of perfecting the technique for underglaze painting, known since the Tang dynasty but not widely used, of applying the design directly on the unfired clay body and covering it with clear glaze before firing.

Blue and white designs had been made since the Yuan dynasty. In Ming they were created with smalt blue known as "Moslem blue" imported from Persia, and styles of designs varied from period to period. With blue and white, Jingdezhen reached its height, becoming known as the porcelain capital of China, and even of the world. The town's fame was such that it even figured in the American poet Henry Wadsworth Longfellow's 1878 poem "Keramos" (a godlike potter, a creation of the author).

Soon it became possible to use red and other colors. In late Ming and in the Qing dynasty which followed, tea porcelain blossomed out in a myriad of colored designs applied by both the underglaze and the later overglaze method. Many of the ancient types of ceramics, long gone except as collectors' items, are now being manufactured again.

TEA THINGS IN MODERN CHINA

Fairly small handleless cups are used, along with those with handles. For all-day drinking, the preferred vessel is a tall mug about twice the size of a standard cup, with a matching lid. While many of these are of very ordinary china, beautifully decorated cups are treasured and enjoyed throughout life. Covered mugs of reddish brown Yixing stoneware, inexpensive, practical, and artistic, are popular.

Drinking glasses, of very thin material so they do not crack even when hot water is poured in, have also been used in recent decades. Some think this is the influence of the Russian tea glass. The difference is that the Russian glass rests in a wrought silver frame with a handle. Any hapless drinker who in a hurry for his tea has burned his fingers on an unclad Chinese glass may wonder whether this is an improvement.

Why do Russians use glasses? Alexandre Dumas, whose prolific nineteenth-century writing extended far beyond novels like *The Three Musketeers*, gives a legend in his *Histoire de la Cuisine* (translated as *Dictionary of Cuisine*). The first Russian teacups bore a view of the city of Kronstadt, where they were made. A teahouse customer, feeling the

Yixing pots are not molded on a wheel but by hand.

drink was too weak, would complain, "I can see Kronstadt." Teahouses began substituting glasses, which showed exactly how strong the tea was.

The one advantage of glasses is aesthetic, because they make it possible to enjoy the floating world created by certain kinds of tea leaves as they unfold. With this criterion alone in mind, glasses might be recommended particularly for Gunpowder, Lung Ching, Baihao Yinzhen (White tea), Yinzhen, and Qiangang Huibai.

PORCELAIN FOR THE WEST

Marco Polo gave Europe its first description of porcelain in his *Travels* published in 1477. He saw it being made in the city of Taicheu in Fujian province, and St. Mark's Cathedral in Venice preserves a small porcelain bottle said to have been brought back by him. The term "porcelain" probably originates with Polo, who had seen cowrie shells (Italian: *porceletta*—piglets) used as money in Tingzhou (today's Changting in western Fujian). Their likeness to this ceramic must have prompted him to coin the word *porcellana*.

Chinese porcelain had been reaching the Middle East by sea, and the east coast of the Mediterranean by camel via the Silk Road since Tang times. Some pieces had been presented to European rulers: the Florentine Lorenzo de' Medici had acquired many by the time he died in 1492.

Collecting and even use of porcelain from the Orient was in vogue among the rich in sixteenth century Italy. Some pieces may have come by way of Portugal, for mariners of that country had reached China and begun trade in 1517. That century saw several attempts to duplicate Ming blue and white in the tin-glazed earthenware of the time (majolica and faience) and in opaque glass, but the results, no matter how beautiful—and deceptive at first sight—were not hard like porcelain.

Early in the 1600s the Dutch captured some Portugese ships, and when the goods were sold in Amsterdam, people marveled at the translucent Chinese porcelain. After gaining a foothold in Taiwan (Formosa) in 1624, the Dutch became the leading world shipper of Chinese porcelain. Dutch potters, probably having seen a few pieces

Blue-and-white designs are still popular for daily-use mugs.

that had come through Java, were already making a blue-and-white stoneware at Delft by methods learned from Italy. The name "China-ware" attached itself to this new thing in English (its original "cheney ware" first appeared in print in 1634), and later came to be applied to all ceramics.

How to make porcelain remained a mystery. A common view was that it demanded a lime mixture aged underground for a century. Dr. Johnson's dictionary even declared that the name porcelain came from the words *pour cent annes* (for a hundred years).

Phoenix-headed wine jug in Ming blue and white porcelain.

EUROPE FINDS THE SECRET

Now enter tea, first brought to Europe by the Dutch in 1610, and widely popular in their country by 1675. Tea as an art needed artistic tea things, so porcelain was in demand not only as art but as tea service. Potters all over Europe sought to unearth the secret of porcelain production, for none of the imitations stood up well to boiling water. It is not surprising therefore, that when porcelain was finally achieved in Europe, the first product was a teapot.

Credited as its creator is Johann-Friedrich Boettger, a druggist's apprentice and alchemist. In trouble in Prussia for failing to change base metal to gold as promised, he had sought refuge in Saxony. Instead of sending Boettger back, as the Prussians demanded, the Elector of Saxony, Augustus II, put him to work with the alchemist E. W. von Tschirnhaus. The latter, needing a crucible that could stand high heat, had collected local clays, and believed that Saxony had materials for producing porcelain. Boettger actually located kaolin by lucky accident. A blacksmith who had found some in a horse's hoof was selling it at the court as a powder for white wigs.

The two alchemists achieved a hard-paste red porcelain in 1703 and white porcelain in 1710. Augustus made Boettger head of Europe's first porcelain factory at Meissen, a village near Dresden. Its tea sets and Dresden (Meissen) china figurines became known worldwide.

Tea utensils spurred the development of numerous porcelain factories on the continent under various royal patronages. The most famous of these in France was Sevres, backed by Madame de Pompadour, mistress of Louis XV. Its most characteristic pieces have an elaborate painted, enameled, and gilded polychrome style of decoration on a dark blue ground.

By the mid-eighteenth century England had seen the rise of many potteries funded by private entrepreneurs, but true porcelain was not produced until the 1760s, in a factory at Plymouth (maker of Bristol china after its move to that town). Tea things were their mainstay and much early decoration was of the type found on Chinese blue and white.

THE BLUE WILLOW PATTERN

After the 1780s a lot of teaware was made of bone china, an English invention made by adding bone ashes to the original porcelain materials. The greatest came from the Wedgewood and Spode potteries. The former produced only tea things—decorated with Chinese and Japanese designs and romantic English landscapes. Spode produced many blue-and-white Chinese patterns (Two Temples and Buffalo, for instance, and many landscapes), but is most famous for its Blue Willow pattern.

This familiar design which has symbolized China for people in many parts of the world is still made today worldwide and in China. It is found on tea sets, but shows to best advantage on plates and dinnerware of all kinds (to the extent that it avoids being trite only by being suffused with a glow of childhood memories). Strangely enough, this exact pattern was not first produced in China. It appeared on Spode ware in 1790, developed out of earlier English designs using both Chinese and Japanese motifs (something resembling it without all the elements had been a standard design in porcelain from China before that time). These include a willow and some fantastic flora, a pillared, upturned-eave building (one is pictured on a shard of Chinese pottery excavated at the Spode factory in 1969), a bridge with three figures running across it (also found on authentic Chinese bowls), a boat, and two birds, all of which appear in relation to each other in many variations.

Blue willow plate.

The popular story about them seems to have been compiled in Britain and the United States *after* the chinaware was already well known, according to Mary Frank Gaston in *Blue Willow*, a book for collectors. There are many variations, involving elements that do appear in numerous Chinese tales, both folk and literary. An "official" version was published by England's Wedgewood potteries, another producer of Blue Willow.

A young woman falls in love with her father's secretary. He is banned from the home, but floats messages to her on a stream that runs under the wall. She does not want to marry the wealthy old man her father has chosen. At the betrothal party her lover slips in as a beggar and they flee over the bridge with the father in pursuit (she holding a distaff, symbol of virginity, he the box of betrothal jewels, and the father a whip). They go to an island, where he farms and writes. His fame spreads and reaches the old man, who sends soldiers to find them and kill the husband. The young woman then takes her own life. Guan Yin, the Goddess of Mercy, pities the lovers and causes their spirits to live on as two white doves (two tragic lovers become butterflies in a well-known Chinese legend).

EIGHTEENTH CENTURY PORCELAIN TRADE

Through the eighteenth century, the rise of the tea vogue in the West stimulated its purchases of Chinese export porcelain. Chinaware, heavy and not damaged by water in the hold, was ideal ballast beneath the lighter bales of silk and wooden chests of tea. One British vessel in 1705 had ten tons of chinaware to 100 tons of tea, 30 of silk, and 35 of copper and other goods, according to a list in Paul Atterbury's *The History of Porcelain*. Sold very cheaply in England, this porcelain helped satisfy the demand for tea things.

Probably few for whom Blue Willow symbolized the faraway Orient fully realized the enormous distance their tea things had come. In addition to the sea voyage around the bottom of Africa, porcelain, like tea, made a long inland journey before reaching the trading ports. From Jingdezhen it was 600 miles, first by boat to the Gan River at Nanchang, then south up the Gan, to be carried over mountains to another river leading to the port of Guangzhou. Another route was by boat to Nanjing on the Yangtze, down that river, and down the coast to Guangzhou.

In London, cups, first for chocolate and coffee, later for tea, were bestsellers. Figures for the three decades between 1690 and 1720 show them brought to Britain in the hundreds of thousands. Next in importance were teapots, then quite small because of the high price of tea. They were of two kinds, with handles either over the top or at the side. Letters from importers demanded a straight, non-clogging spout for easy pouring, with a sieve at its base to hold in the leaves. After 1728 most pots for Britain had these features.

The earliest European tea must have been drunk from handleless bowls, and indeed the usage "dish of tea" continued into the nineteenth century and beyond. Yet diarist Pepys records in 1660 that he had a *cup* of tea. The British had long had a handled cup for posset (hot milk with an alcoholic addition) so export pressures put handles on Chinese teacups for Britain and to some extent China too. Handled and handleless cups were used side by side through the eighteenth century. As tea grew less costly, cups grew larger, to today's size.

A remarkable aspect of this century to which little attention has been paid in China itself is the degree of adaptation and production organization the Chinese manufacturers developed in order to satisfy the demands of bulk buyers like the Dutch and British East India companies, and private sellers like their captains and other functionaries. "Chinese export porcelain" is now prized by collectors, and numerous books for them give an idea of the varied designs made especially for the foreign market.

In addition to Chinese designs adapted to buyers' demands, porcelain sets featured some in the Western idiom, often done abroad. These included landscapes, figures both legendary and contemporary, coats of arms, commemoratives of Western events. There were also many drawings by Chinese artists of port scenes, the traders' ships, and their Chinese workshops in action. Famous in American history are the dinner sets with the emblem of the Society of Cincinnatus formed by veterans of the Revolutionary War. They were commissioned in 1784 by the captain of the *Empress of China*, the first vessel from the new

United States to sail to China. George Washington purchased 302 pieces.

As the century neared its end, the porcelain trade with Britain dropped off. Native British production of chinaware was rising, and in the 1760s the use of underglaze transfer patterns from paper eliminated laborious hand painting and speeded up manufacture, thus making possible greater production. It seems hard to believe that this was not already being done in China, as one stage of the process employs stencils much like Chinese papercuts.

The British East India Company decided in 1779 to order no more porcelain from China, although private sales continued. But imports of tea kept on rising, and tea things were still in demand. This gave the British ceramics industry an open road to development, often with the Chinese designs the public had come to know and love.

CADDIES, ETC., JAPAN AND ELSEWHERE

Sharing in the story of tea ceramics along with cups, saucers, and pots were sugar bowls and creamers for the West, a "teapot stand" or plate on which the pot stood, a jar for waste water, and tea caddies. In China these latter were most often small, round, full-bellied covered jars. They shared all the artistry of whatever ceramic trend was popular, but the Chinese seem to have to considered chiefly their utilitarian aspect as a vessel for storing tea. Caddies made for the West, whether or not part

A lively street market business goes on in Jingdezhen, China's porcelain capital.

of a set, were often works of art and frequently trimmed with silver. Some were boxes with containers for two kinds of tea and, because of the price of the leaves, with provision for a lock.

In Japan the tea caddy became an extremely important part of the tea ceremony, to be displayed before the event, and examined and admired by guests at the proper time during it. The leaves were stored in much larger jars and placed in these quite small caddies after they had been ground to a powder. Caddies of lacquerware had their day, but ceramic caddies came to rank as works of art, listed right after calligraphy and painting in sixteenth century Japan. They are still made today with beautiful decoration and in fanciful shapes—as a gnarled piece of wood, for example.

SILVER TEA SERVICE

That silver was a material eminently suited to a hot, acidic liquid like tea was already known by Lu Yu, who may have boiled his tea in a silver vessel. Western aristocrats discovered this not long after taking to tea, and in 1678 a large "Silver Tea-Pott," inscribed as such, was presented to the British East India Company, said to be the first one known in the West.

Pots made in subsequent decades and called after England's Queen Anne, were pear-shaped, that is, larger on the bottom. Each came with a hinged lid and rested on a pedestal to keep the heat off the table. By the end of the eighteenth century the pear had been inverted, and later an oval shape was introduced. Silver teapots were created with decoration in ornate baroque or trim classical style as each current fashion demanded. Similar styles were produced in the American colonies. One of the best silver craftsmen was the famed rider of the revolution, Paul Revere.

Spoons, trays, sugar tongs, and trivets for tea use were all manufactured in great quantities. The process of making Sheffield plate developed in the 1840s (silver over a sheet of copper). From it parts could be stamped out, and it paved the way to mass production of silver-plated tea things by 1800.

SEVEN

🌿 Tea Growing and Processing

T he tea plant, an evergreen with small, white rose-like blooms that
have also been likened to apple blossoms, is indigenous to China,
Tibet and northern India. Lu Yu's classic mentions a wild tea tree in
Sichuan that needed two men with arms outstretched to encircle its
trunk. In recent times many such wild trees towering up to forty feet
have been found in southern and eastern Sichuan, and in Yunnan and
Guizhou provinces along the lower reaches of the Lancang, Nu, Qu,
Pan, and Hongshui rivers.

A King Tea Tree judged to be over 1,700 years old is still growing in
the forested Xishuangbanna region of Yunnan province near the Burma
border. It is 108 feet (32 meters) tall, with the main trunk over a yard in
diameter. When left to grow uncared for, tea plants can exceed 30 feet.
To maintain a manageable height, tea growers prune them down to two
or three feet.

The genus *Camellia*, to which the tea plant belongs, is a very old one
dating from the Tertiary period, which preceded the great ice ages. The
plant was able to survive because the Yunnan and Guizhou plateaus were
not affected by the glaciation.

The tea plant gained generic status of its own in the West in 1753 in
the plant classification *Species Plantarium* by the famous Swedish botanist Carl von Linne (Linnaeus). He called it *Thea sinensis*, Chinese tea,
and believed that green tea and black tea came from two different plants.
Today this is known to be untrue: they come from the same plant. There

are, however, subdivisions, for different types developed from the original, which is believed to have been a large-leaved tree.

However, to compound the confusion, while there are not many varieties of plants, the variety of teas abounds. They reflect various strains, differences in topography, soil, and climate in diverse tea growing districts, and methods of processing. Authorities have cited between 350 and 500 varieties of teas. The prominent nineteenth century British botanist Sir George Watt defined four varieties of the tea plant, but most tea growers acknowledge only three, named for location: China, Assam, and Cambodia. The contemporary scientist J. R. Sealy says there are two, China and Assam. The Chinese classification of three differs little from the Western one.

In the Western classification, the China type is considered to be a bush, not a tree, mainly because it is multi-stemmed, though it can be fifteen feet high. It grows at high elevations, can stand cold winters, and produces for a hundred years, twice as long as other varieties. The leaves, about two inches in length, are the smallest of the three varieties, and are serrated and rather hard.

What's in a Name?

The scientific name for tea has been a matter of confusion. Some books list the plant as named by the famous Swedish botanist Linnaeus, *Thea sinensis*, because according to the International Rules of Nomenclature, the first name given a new species is always maintained. Other call it *Camellia sinensis*, relying on the studies of the prominent nineteenth-century botanist Sir George Watt, who on the basis of location and leaf and tree size concluded that it was a species of the genus *Camellia*. A 1958 study considered to be the definitive one on the taxonomy of tea, *A Revision of the Genus Camellia*, by J. R. Sealy, holds that the tea plant is an evergreen tree or shrub with eighty-one species, five of which are related to the tea plant. He calls it *Camellia sinensis*, and this is generally accepted as the standard today.

The Assam type, because it is single-stemmed, is considered a tree, and can reach a height of forty-five to sixty feet. The leaves range from six to fourteen inches in length. One of its subvarieties is the dark-leafed Assam which grows at high altitudes at Darjeeling, India. The fine down on its leaves gives its product the name Gold Tipped Darjeeling, considered to have a very delicate flavor and known as "the champagne of teas." The large-leafed trees that grow in China's Yunnan province are of the Assam type.

The Cambodian type, growing to about fifteen feet, is also considered a tree, and is used mainly to cross with other varieties. The Chinese classifications are (not in exactly the same order) bush, tree-bush and tree.

Scientists currently believe that all of the different types of tea descended from one center, probably located near the source of the Irrawaddy River in Burma, and gradually spread throughout Southeast Asia in a fanlike movement.

Tea is grown commercially in a belt that circles the earth on either side of the equator. "Superior tea comes from high mountains," is an old Chinese saying, but the best places lie in mountains below 6,000 feet. The altitude and mountain mists help protect against excessive sunlight and create the right temperature and humidity to enable the leaves and buds to develop slowly and remain tender. Thus they produce a higher content of caffeine, amino acids, and essential oils. The frost, heat, and dampness of the lowlands are not conducive to good growth. At a daily mean temperature above 68 degrees Fahrenheit (20 degrees centigrade) the buds are rough and age rapidly.

Many of China's most famous teas come from well-known mountains: Wuyi (Fujian), Lushan (Jiangxi), Emei (Sichuan), and Huangshan (Anhui). Tea plants grow best in an acid soil of pH4.5 to 6.5 with a moisture content of 70 to 80 percent, and air humidity above 70 percent.

Tea has been cultivated commercially in China for at least eighteen hundred years and in Japan since 800 A.D. It grows from Hainan in the remote south as far north as Shandong province in more than a thousand counties in seventeen provinces (Anhui, Fujian, Gansu, Guangdong, Guizhou, Hainan, Henan, Hubei, Hunan, Jiangsu, Jiangxi, Shaanxi, Shandong, Sichuan, Taiwan, Yunnan, and Zhejiang) and the Tibet and

Tea terraces, Anxi county,

Fujian province.

Guangxi Zhuang autonomous regions. Zhejiang, Hunan, and Sichuan rank first in order of importance, and Anhui and Fujian are also big producers. South of the Yangtze River, tea plucking can go on for seven months a year, and on Hainan Island, all year round.

HOW TEA GROWS

Traditionally, tea plants were grown from seeds the size of hazelnuts, gathered in October and kept over the winter in a mixture of sand and earth. With this method, in spring they are sown either in a nursery area or directly into the field, about four feet apart. After two years the plants, now five to six feet tall, are cut back to about one foot. They are allowed to grow a bit, but after that are pruned weekly to keep them waist high. Plucking can begin at three years, or at five in high altitudes. A bush can produce for thirty or forty years.

Plants can also be started from cuttings or through layering, that is, transplanting of rooted branches. The years since the 1960s have seen cloning, which involves a leaf cutting rather than a branch cutting. The layering and cutting methods are the only ones that yield a true reproduction of a strain, as a plant that grows from seed may be the result of cross-fertilization and unlike either of its parents.

Most tea plants have a flush, or growth, period and a dormant phase. The leaves are plucked when the young shoots, or flush, are coming out. In the hotter climates the plants have several flushes and leaves can be plucked all year round. At higher elevations, there is a distinct plucking season. In most parts of China, harvesting takes place from April to October. Plucking in northern India and Japan is also seasonal.

Leaves from the earlier flushes, usually in spring, are considered the most desirable, with the second flush the best of all. The reason for this is that the sunlight is milder in the spring than in summer or fall. The choice parts to be plucked are the "two leaves and a bud" (the first two leaves and the bud at the tip), a poetic phrase which was used as the title of a fine novel by the Indian writer Mulk Raj Anand. They are nipped off by the thumbnail with a downward movement of the thumb. The leaf bud is considered the finest quality, partly for the fine hair, or tip, on the end and underside of the leaf. This, the pekoe (in Chinese *bai hao* or white hair), is what imparts the finest flavor to the tea. The more white down the better.

Plucking and pruning take a great deal of labor, and labor is listed with acid soil and adequate rainfall as one of the three things necessary for growing tea. In India tea cultivation started on large estates which more easily lent themselves to mechanization. In China tea was produced mainly on small family plots, often in the hills where mechanized cultivation was difficult.

China is one of the few countries in the world still considered to have land that can be opened for tea growing, and large state tea farms as well as smaller plots have been established on unused land. Picking remains one major operation that has never been successfully mechanized, as skilled fingers have not been successfully replaced. Although picking is still done by expert hands, these farms are highly mechanized in other respects, even so far as use of spray irrigation.

A basketful, Anxi, Fujian province.

THE PROCESSING DIFFERENCE

Green tea and black tea come from the same plant. Although certain strains of that plant are preferred for each type, the chief difference lies in processing. The main types of tea are black, which undergoes a process of oxidation, called fermentation; oolong, which is oxidized about half as long (semi-fermented); and green tea, which is not fermented. This process should really be called oxidation, for that is what happens to the leaves. They are not fermented, or worked on by biological microorganisms.

What in the West is known as black tea is "red tea," *hongcha*, in China. Some authorities say the name derives from the red edges on the leaves after fermentation, while others claim it refers to the red tint of certain black teas when brewed, such as the "Keemun Red" tea. Mainly green tea is drunk by Chinese, whether in or outside China.

Black Tea

The process for making black tea is said to have been learned from that for making oolong tea, or rather is an extension of it. The traditional method of processing black tea involves four basic steps: withering, rolling (for *gongfu* only), fermenting, and drying (firing, de-enzymizing).

First the leaves are spread out in the open for several hours on bamboo trays—in the shade for the finer grades—to be wilted until they are limp enough to be rolled without cracking. When they reach this point they give out a fruity, apple-like fragrance.

The next step is rolling, sometimes preceded by repeated tossing of the leaves in baskets. Rolling used to be done by hand between the palms or against bamboo trays, with a worker going over the tray as many as three to four hundred times. The purpose is to bruise the leaves, breaking down their membranes to bring together the chemical substances called catechins and the enzyme polyphenolase (polyphenol oxidase) which activates the oxidation of the former. After rolling, the lumps of leaves must be separated by a roll breaker.

Two leaves and a bud, Anxi.

Rolling the leaves gives them their future form. The two main characteristics of a cup of black tea are its flavor, accompanied by color, and the particular effect of the polyphenols, called pungency or astringency. A twisted leaf releases less pungency and more flavor during infusion, and does it over a longer time, thus achieving a more even balance between the two.

Fermentation or oxidation goes on for several hours while the leaves are spread out in a cool place. The leaves absorb oxygen which activates enzymes to create essential oils and causes chemical changes, oxidizing some of the polyphenols, or what is known as the tannin. Leaves oxidized longer produce tea with more color but less flavor. During the process, leaves begin to turn red around the edges and to give off a fragrance like almonds.

Firing, almost like stir-frying, is traditionally carried out in a large metal wok over a very hot fire. It stops the enzyme action, sterilizes the leaves, and stops the fermentation process. Now this step can be done in large ovens with temperatures up to 194 degrees Fahrenheit (90 degrees centigrade). Often the thicker, high-quality leaves alternate several times between the fermentation and firing process.

Then the leaves, now 80 percent dry, complete their drying over charcoal or wood fires. The last step is to sift the leaves to sort by size. It is important that the size be uniform in each grade. Otherwise, as smaller pieces infuse more quickly, uniform strength for each grade could not be guaranteed. There are two main categories: the leaf grade, *(gongfu)* and the broken grade used in teabags. The latter produces a dark, strong brew more quickly. Fannings, one of its subdivisions, is widely used in tea bags. A still finer sorting too small for tea bags is called "dust" and used in tea bricks and tablets.

The process of black tea manufacture may seem finished, but there is one more step—blending to ensure a brand of consistent quality. This is done by the big tea packers such as Lipton. Most name brand black teas are blends and may include as many as twenty or thirty teas from two or three countries.

Keemun (see p. 147) is the best known of China's black teas. China exports 90 percent of her black tea production, for green and oolong are preferred inside China.

Picking out the twigs, Anxi.

Oolong Tea

Because they are to produce a full-bodied beverage, the leaves for oolong must not be picked too early or at too tender a stage, but just when they reach their peak. They must be processed immediately. Unlike leaves for green tea, those destined to be oolong are wilted in direct sunlight. Then they are shaken in tubular bamboo baskets to bruise the leaf edges. This bruising is what makes the edges oxidize faster than the center.

The leaves are alternately shaken and spread out to air-dry several times until the veins become transparent and the leaf surface yellows. The edges become reddish as a result of oxidation, while the center remains green, and the leaves give off an orchid-like fragrance. The fermentation is arrested halfway through by firing. The temperature for oolong is higher than for other teas. The final product contains less moisture, which enables it to keep longer.

Oolong is produced in Fujian, the province of its origin, and some other mainland provinces. The technique for processing it was taken by Fukienese migrants to Taiwan, and that island's Tungting (Dongding) oolong is well known. There may be some difference among mainland and Taiwanese oolongs in taste and medicinal function, due to different soil, processing, and fermentation time. Oolongs from the mainland are said to have more body, the result of longer oxidation, than those from Taiwan. Oolong is the tea most often served in Chinese restaurants in the United States and south China.

Green Tea

The leaves for green tea may or may not be withered first. Then they are de-enzymized by panfrying. Ninety percent are done this way. Five percent are treated by steaming to make the leaves soft, and about the same amount are baked. Then comes rolling and firing, often alternately. The leaves turn a yellow-green. There is no fermentation, hence no chemical change.

Mechanization of processing began on the Indian tea estates in the late nineteenth century with hot air firing, rolling by a moving box that fed leaves onto a flat surface, mechanical sorting, and now machines which combine some steps, thus taking much less time. In China, collective farming beginning in the 1950s stimulated mechanization. Early semi-mechanization included things like a mechanical arm to stir the leaves being fired in the large wok. Some state tea farms have been set up with a fair degree of mechanization in processing. Smaller producers bring their leaf to local factories which are generally well equipped.

The finest teas, however, are still hand-processed. The traditional skill, like that of a handicraft, has been passed down through the generations—the understanding of the relation of the heat to the condition of leaves to obtain the desired effect, the hand movements in relation to heat, the special way of shaping certain kinds, for instance Lu'an Guapian (Lu'an Melon Seeds), Gunpowder, and Lung Ching. This makes the product more costly, but the aesthetic appearance of the processed leaves is part of the art of enjoying tea. This is so highly valued that many Chinese prefer to pay more for their tea, even if it means having tea less often.

The five best known Chinese green teas (see list p. 124) are Lung Ching, Huangshan Mao Feng, Pi Lo Chun, Puto Fo Cha, and Lu'an Guapian.

China is the world's largest exporter of green tea, supplying 90 percent of that sold on the international market. Zhejiang province is a big producer. Of every two cups of green tea poured outside China, one is from Zhejiang, according to an official of the Zhejiang Tea Branch of the state-run China National Native Produce and Animal Byproducts Import and Export Corporation.

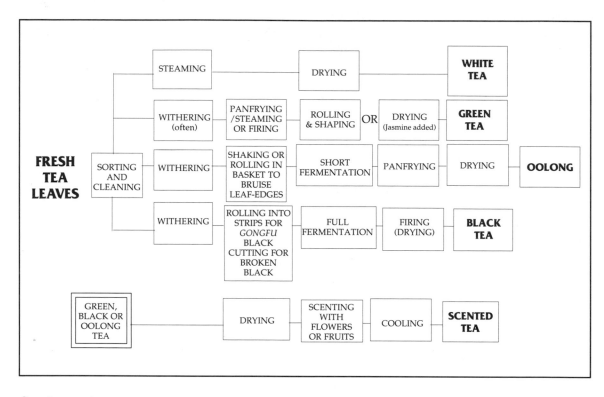

Steps in processing.

EIGHT 🍃 *Some Tea Chemistry*

W hen you pour boiling water over black or oolong tea leaves you are releasing the results of some truly wonderful chemical developments that occur during the processing, which is known as fermentation. Green tea is not fermented.

The three most important chemical substances in the fresh tea leaf are caffeine, aromatic or essential oils, and polyphenols (popularly but incorrectly known as tannins). Caffeine, found in many plants in nature, will be discussed more fully in the following chapter. The essential oils are important constituents of the aroma of the beverage. These substances are sometimes known as volatiles, which means that they will totally evaporate in strong heat. When tea is kept a long time, these disappear, reducing aroma. Both tannins and oils aid digestion by stimulating peristalsis of the intestinal tract. There is some evidence that tea counteracts the effect of fats by emulsifying them in the digestive tract. The polyphenols are the most interesting elements and the ones which do the greatest good for human health.

During manufacture, black and oolong tea undergo their fermentation process (for details see pp. 82–84). Spread out in a cool place, the leaves absorb oxygen, which creates chemical changes. This process should correctly be called oxidation, for the leaves are worked on by oxygen rather than fermented by microorganisms.

The polyphenols, about thirty altogether, account for nearly a third of the soluble matter in the fresh tea leaf. During the fermentation process about a third (some say half) of the total amount is oxidized into more complicated oxidized products such as theaflavin. Therefore, after this process the tea contains two kinds of polyphenols, oxidized and unoxidized (natural polyphenols). The latter, released in the beverage, create the astringent, "puckery" feeling in the mouth when you drink tea. This stimulates the salivary glands, which is why tea is a thirst quencher.

The unoxidized polyphenols provide the pungency, while the oxidized ones give the tea its color and flavor. The higher the degree of oxidation, the more color and less pungency a tea has. Green tea, which does not undergo oxidation, has more natural unoxidized polyphenols, and also

---

"Tannin,"
Another Misnomer

Tea polyphenols, though popularly known as tannins, are not, as widely believed, the tannic acid used in leather preparation. In fact, they are not tannins at all. With some chemical and functional similarity, they became known by this name long before modern methods of chemical analysis made it possible to distinguish the two.

Here we have run into another of those name confusions that seem to haunt tea. There's more. Three-fourths of the tea polyphenols are catechins which are part of the chemical group flavanols (they do indeed have something to do with flavor, as distinct from either aroma or astringency). At least six catechins have been isolated.

We might make a summary outline like this:

Polyphenols (compounds with two or more phenolic hydroxyl groups)

Flavanols (one kind of polyphenol)

Catechins (the name for flavanols in tea)

Reports on the health benefits of these substances may use any of the three. Often no distinction is made between the terms "catechins" and "polyphenols," and in many cases the two are used interchangeably.

more astringency. Black tea has more color but less astringency. Both oxidizied and unoxidized polyphenols may be beneficial.

Now let's see what happens in the polyphenol oxidation process. At the tea factory, the freshly picked leaves sit until they have become soft and limp as a result of water evaporation. Then they are rolled to break down the membranes and bring the juices containing polyphenols in contact with the enzyme polyphenolase (polyphenol oxidase) which catalyzes the oxidation of the polyphenols by oxygen in the atmosphere. The product resulting from this process, together with other constituents, accounts for the unique flavor and rich, deeper color of black and oolong teas.

The action of the enzyme, and therefore the oxidation process, is eventually stopped through heating, but these compounds remain in the dried prepared leaves waiting for the boiling water to dissolve them.

MILK, SUGAR, LEMON

Milk, sugar, or lemon are frequently added by black tea drinkers of the Western world. For those accustomed to it, milk seems to add to the comfort of a cup of tea.

However, the polyphenols in tea also bind with milk protein. Therefore, does putting milk into black tea cut down the effects of its polyphenols? Not substantially, says Professor Chi-tang Ho of Rutgers University, who has done considerable research on tea chemistry. Even in black tea, which has been fermented, about 30 percent of the polyphenols remain unoxydized, and the milk combines first with the 70 percent of oxidized polyphenols, and the chief effect is to ease their harshness to your stomach. So if you prefer the taste of black tea, milk is probably a good thing. However, if you put in too much milk, when it has finished with the oxydized polyphenols, it will go on to the unoxydized ones.

Neither sugar nor lemon juice had until recently been thought to have any effect on the chemistry of tea. However, researchers at the University of Wisconsin found that adding the enzyme tannase, or lemon juice, to black tea increased iron and calcium solubility, and therefore absorption by the body. The polyphenols can bind with iron and calcium, preventing these minerals from being absorbed, but lemon juice inhibits this binding, keeping the minerals available.

In the 1950s it was learned that when lemon tea was served in styrofoam containers the polystyrene dissolved into the beverage. It should never be served in these containers.

Artificial sweeteners, or sugar substitutes, are safe with tea, according to Professor Ho. They do not create any chemical reaction.

VITAMIN C AND OTHER NUTRIENTS

In China it is widely stated that tea (green) is a source of vitamin C. Since this vitamin is destroyed by heat and tea is made in hot water, this statement seems contradictory. Recent tests in China found that heat destruction does occur, but not in tea. Something in tea, as yet undetermined, apparently helps stabilize vitamin C.

The amount of vitamin C varies greatly depending on growing conditions, the age of the leaves at picking, and how long they have been stored. Japanese tests found that tea stored three years had lost all its vitamin C. According to Chinese calculations, typical green tea made with three grams (one teaspoonful) of dry leaves to a cup should yield about six milligrams of of the total content of vitamin C in three infusions in water at 158 to 212 degrees Fahrenheit (70 to 100 degrees centigrade). Eighty-five percent of the vitamin C is released in one five-minute infusion at 176 degrees Fahrenheit (80 degrees centigrade). As for black tea, authorities have long believed that almost all its vitamin C is destroyed during fermentation.

Tea also contains vitamins B_1, B_2, K, and P, and niacin, folic acid, and manganese, but in such small amounts as to be negligible. A cup of black tea has 58 milligrams of potassium.

NINE 🍃 *Tea and Your Health*

I n Chinese there is a proverb which in literal translation could read:

Drinking a daily cup of tea
Will surely starve the apothec'ry.

Or, to give it a more American ring,

A daily cup of tea or more
Keeps you out of the drugstore.

Only recently has this axiom been tested by modern scientific methods.
Already there is considerable evidence that regular tea drinking can

---

T ea is better than water for it does not carry disease; neither does it act like poison as water does when the wells contain foul and rotten matter.

Shen Nong's Canon of Medicinal Herbs

benefit health, as the Chinese learned through thousands of years of experience.

The most elementary reason tea has saved millions of lives over two thousand years is simply because making it requires boiling water, which kills disease germs. In areas of poor water quality, every cup of tea was one less of hazardous water.

THREE MAIN COMPONENTS

The three main components of the tea leaf are caffeine, polyphenols (popularly but incorrectly known as tannins), and aromatic or essential oils. Here in brief is what they do. *Caffeine*, in moderate quantities, stimulates the central nervous system and promotes blood circulation. It stimulates the process of elimination and acts as a diuretic promoting better kidney function. There is some evidence that regular tea drinkers have a lower incidence of kidney ailments and gallstones. Some researchers have even claimed that it also helps the body excrete radioactive strontium 90, the element which entered the food chain from atmospheric fallout from nuclear bomb testing.

Polyphenols isolated from tea (see chapter eight) may act as an anticancer agent in that they have an antimutant factor which helps cell DNA to reproduce itself accurately rather than in mutated forms which might lead to cancer. Medicines made from tea polyphenols have become part of the treatment for nephritis, chronic hepatitis, and leukemia in China. The *essential oils* (sometimes called aromatic oils, sometimes volatiles because they totally evaporate) are formed in the tea leaves as they grow. They account for the aroma of the beverage. These substances also aid digestion and help emulsify fat. Green tea has more essential oils than the more highly processed black tea. That is why black tea has less aroma. Jasmine tea is said to have the greatest amount, ranging from .06 percent to .4 percent. Some of this may come from the jasmine blossoms.

RESULTS OF RESEARCH

Some of the recent findings in tea research have been presented at international conferences, the largest of which was the six-day International Tea Quality/Human Health Symposium held in Hangzhou, China, in November 1987. Sponsored by the Tea Research Institute under the Chinese Academy of Agricultural Sciences, it received 105 papers from scientists in eleven countries. Twenty-five of those dealing with health were published, along with some others, in booklet form. Their results were reaffirmed and augmented in reports at a meeting of Chinese medical and tea scientists in Beijing in November 1989. Smaller conferences have met in France and elsewhere. The sampling of the findings below indicates some of the points that have been made about the relation between tea and health.

The research so far has been scattered and unsystematic in that each group seems to investigate what interests it without any comprehensive plan. Reports are fragmentary, results are sometimes contradictory, and methodology varies. It is often impossible to compare studies on the efficacy of the various kinds of teas because different criteria were used in evaluating them. For instance, we learn that Jasmine tea "markedly

---

Tea came to the West with guarantees of health. The first known mention of it outside the Orient was by a Muslim traveler named Sulieman. His description of it as a widely used Chinese beverage considered "very wholesome" did not attract attention in ninth century Europe, which had its own problems. By the time tea was mentioned again, the Age of Exploration had brought about greater receptivity—and interest in tea as a possible trade product.

In 1559 a three-volume work appeared, compiled by Giambattista Ramusio, secretary of the Council of Venice, whose duties included meeting travelers and gathering information for trade. This *Navigatione e Viaggi* quotes the Persian merchant Hajji Mahomet's statement to Ramusio that tea was used in China against fever, headache, upset stomach, and other ailments. His observation: the Chinese say that if Persia and lands westward learn about tea, their merchants

Tea's Healthful Virtues Win Europe

enhanced" the cell immune function of rats, but we do not know why Jasmine tea was chosen, what it is in the tea that produces this effect, or whether ordinary green tea without the presence of jasmine blossoms would produce the same results.

A STIMULANT AND THE FLAP ABOUT CAFFEINE

The victory over fatigue that tea provides is a big reason for its popularity. Caffeine is what does it, and caffeine has been a matter of controversy. A stimulant, caffeine has been shown to speed reaction time, increase alertness, and improve concentration.

The original intake of caffeine causes the body to create stimulant

---

will stop buying rhubarb (rhubarb for medicinal use had been a classic Chinese export).

Mention of tea in China was included in a 1589 book on India written for Jesuit missionaries. Tea protected the people from "pituitary troubles, heaviness in the head, and ailments of the eyes; it conduces to a long life almost free of languor," the book said. The first printed reference to tea in English may be a description of the serving of tea, and its esteem, in Japan in a 1598 edition of a travel narrative by the Dutch Jan Huighen van Lindschooten.

Father Matteo Ricci, the famed Jesuit missionary at the Ming dynasty court, said that tea drinking contributed to longevity and freedom from serious illnesses among the Chinese. His journals appeared in English in 1610 and his opinion was reaffirmed by published writings of other Jesuits.

A member of a Dutch East India Company group visiting the Chinese emperor in 1655 was more specific. John Nieuhoff wrote that the greatest beneficiaries of tea were those who had overindulged in food or drink. He cited various Chinese praises for tea and the belief that it prevented kidney stones and gout. From Nieuhoff also comes the only mention of Chinese use of milk in tea (see p. 20).

chemicals, catecholamines, that relay nerve impulses to the brain. The height of this effect lasts from 15 to 45 minutes. After six hours the body has eliminated half of the caffeine.

If this can be described as a spiritual benefit, then the physical effects include stimulation of digestive juice, metabolism, and the kidneys in ways that possibly help eliminate toxins. Also, stimulation of the heart and respiratory system brings more oxygen to the brain, thus increasing mental alertness, shortening reaction time, and improving efficiency of muscle action.

Because there has been much concern in the United States about possible dangers of caffeine, it should be noted that all types of tea contain less caffeine than coffee. Green tea has less than black.

Caffeine tolerance, however, varies greatly among individuals, and an

---

The Chinese experience with tea was filtering to the West, and would soon be added to by European experiments. Not all claims were without exaggeration, and some members of the medical profession objected. Simon Pauli, a German physician, argued in 1635 that though tea might have such good effects in the Orient, it lost this ability in the European climate. He warned that it was dangerous, and hastened death of the drinkers, particularly those over forty. Others, not necessarily doctors, actually claimed that the use of tea would cause Europeans to develop Asiatic features.

Between 1625 and 1657 the Great Tea Debate raged in Holland, and spilled over into France, with medical personages on both sides. Louis XIV's doctor, Lemery, was pro-tea, and had used it to cure Louis' headaches. Louis' prime minister, Cardinal Mazarin, took tea for his gout, and indirectly helped end the debate. M. Cressy, son of a prominent surgeon, researched the beneficial effect of tea on gout and presented his findings on its positive role in a four-hour dissertation at the College of Medicine. After that there were few attacks on tea.

In 1660, Londoners read coffeehouse proprietor Thomas Garway's remarkable handbill describing the benefits of tea to health. It was a excess of it is toxic. Of greater concern is the fact that some research has shown a possibility that caffeine can interfere with fetal development, including lowering birth weight and contributing to skeletal and other abnormalities. Babies cannot get rid of caffeine metabolites until they reach the age of seven or eight months and traces of caffeine can appear in breast milk, also. In light of these concerns, pregnant and nursing mothers should limit or avoid any beverage with caffeine, including tea.

Caffeine content is also affected by the length of the infusion in water:

---

stimulant; helped headache and dizziness; cleared the kidneys, liver, and spleen and prevented stones; settled the stomach and promoted appetite; aided digestion of meat; relaxed the brain and strengthened the memory, to list a few (for text see p. 163).

The seventeenth century had much concern and very little information about health. Hygiene was abysmal. Only one-quarter of the people born lived past the age of twenty-six. For some time, the bubonic plague had ravaged cities on the Continent. It struck England its most brutal blow in the 1665 epidemic. Discoveries of the next half century which would lay the basis for modern medicine—the microscope, theory of blood circulation, blood transfusions, and the germ theory—had not yet been made. Not knowing what to do, people were desperate for remedies, especially during the plague. Coffee too, though initially welcomed to Europe for its flavor and as a stimulant, had been promoted as a cure for gout and scurvy and as the "all-healing berry."

Garway's handbill, however, is not mere high-powered salesmanship. Its assertions involve specific conditions and it does not make empty claims about numerous other health problems of the day. The experience of both China and continental Europe must have been at hand for Garway to draw on. Modern scientific investigation has upheld many of his claims for tea and is continuing to explore ways in which tea might benefit health never dreamed of by Garway and his age.

CAFFEINE CONTENT OF BEVERAGES (5 OZ. CUP)

COFFEE		TEA (black tea assumed)	
Drip	60–180 mg.	Brewed, major U.S. brands	20–80 mg.
Percolator	40–70	Brewed, imported brands	25–110
Instant	30–120	Iced (12 oz.)	67–76
Decaffeinated (brewed)	2–5	Instant	25–50
Decaffeinated (instant)	1–5	OTHER	
		Hot cocoa	2–20 mg.
		Coca Cola (12 oz., reg. or diet) (About medium for cola drinks)	46

Source: Mainly from Denise Grady's, "Don't Get Jittery Over Caffeine" (*Discover*, July 1986) using figures from the U.S. Food and Drug Administration. As beverages vary widely according to the way they are made, these and all other figures are approximate.

A Chinese source suggests 12 milligrams of caffeine per cup of green tea. It gives the caffeine ratio as: black, 3; oolong, 1.5; green, 1. At that rate, taking the above figures, by our calculations the list would read:

Black	25–110 mg.
Oolong	12–55
Green	8–36

*"Tea Emperor" Song
Hui Zong, summarized
by John Blofeld*

Tea induces lightness of spirit, clarity of mind and freedom from all sense of constriction, whether mental or physical; and it promotes such serenity that mundane cares fall away so that whatever is strident or exacerbating in daily life can be put out of mind for a while.

Black tea infused for 5 minutes yields 40–100 milligrams, whereas a 3-minute infusion produces 20–40 milligrams, or half as much. Twenty cups of green tea yield 240 milligrams, or about 12 milligrams per cup, according to Chen Binfan of the Fujian Tea Society.

Tea bags, which contain broken leaves of smaller size, produce an infusion with more caffeine than does loose tea. This is also true of very fine loose tea.

NEWS: CAFFEINE'S NOT SO BAD

The news gets better as we go along. Not only is tea lower in caffeine, but now it's been found that caffeine in moderation is not dangerous.

Numerous studies of caffeine have been made in the United States over the past decade. Most were concerned with coffee, but black tea, as an alternative beverage, has been involved by implication. Some early studies linked caffeine to pancreatic cancer and heart disease, but further recent research does not bear this out. In fact, so far no one has been able to prove any direct relationship between serious illness and beverage caffeine in moderate amounts.

Tests have been unable to pinpoint such a relationship because many other factors must be considered (smoking, stress, lifestyle, diet, etc.). A broad study made in Norway originally stated that heavy coffee drinkers had higher blood cholesterol and triglyceride levels, but a second look showed that many of the subjects smoked, had a high fat consumption, and took insufficient exercise. "Coffee drinking may therefore indicate an unhealthy lifestyle," was the conclusion as reported in the University of California's prestigious *U.C. Berkeley Wellness Newsletter* (July 1988).

The caffeine in coffee or tea drunk in moderation should not harm a healthy person, says the newsletter, or even give rise to the jitters known as coffee nerves. Pregnant women and nursing mothers are urged, however, not to exceed moderation levels, and persons with irregular heartbeats might be better off with no caffeine-containing beverages. Moderation is defined as 200 to 250 milligrams per day, about the equivalent of the caffeine in two cups of coffee. In that case, drinkers of tea, with its lower caffeine content, should have no problem. Physicians have long prescribed caffeine in medicines. Studies are now putting less emphasis on caffeine as a danger and more on its uses to benefit health.

Caffeine stimulates movement of the intestinal tract and increases the flow of digestive juices. This could be one reason why a cup of tea after a greasy meal helps dissipate the fat and alleviates the feeling of discomfort.

TEA AGAINST CANCER

Considerable research is being carried out on the role of tea drinking in preventing cancer. Out of twenty-five papers related to health presented at the Hangzhou Symposium, seven reported on research on cancer and tumors. Green tea seems to get the best results, with Lung Ching preferred.

Stomach cancer, the number one cause of death in Japan, is at its lowest rate in Shizuoka prefecture along the coast southwest of Tokyo.

T ea overcometh superfluous Sleep, and prevents Sleepiness in general . . . so that without trouble whole nights may be spent in study without hurt to the Body.

Garway's Broadsheet, London, 1660

One explanation is that Shizuoka is a tea-growing district and its inhabitants drink large amounts of green tea. This is the conclusion of Professor I. Oguni of Shizuoka University, who did a twelve-year study using government demographic figures.

The study polled people in cities with high and low mortality rates from gastric cancer. In the low mortality areas, it found that people drank tea often and drank it strong. In the high mortality spots they favored weak tea and drank it infrequently, according to research presented by Oguni and others from Hamamatsu College of Shizuoka University and Terumo Corporation, at the Hangzhou Symposium.

Similar findings were reported from a survey in China's Sichuan province in 1986 and another in 1986–1989 in Jiangsu province. The incidence of stomach cancer was found to be remarkably lower in Sichuan areas of heavy tea drinking. Jucha county in Jiangsu, where much tea is drunk, was found to have a lower incidence of liver cancer than Qidong county, where not so much tea is used. (Beijing meeting, November 1989.)

Tea has some effect against cancer because it inhibits the formation or action of cancer-causing substances. Tea may block the action of nitrosamines which can cause cancer, said Dr. Han Chi, an associate professor at the Institute of Nutrition and Food Hygiene under the Chinese Academy of Preventative Medicine. In a test of 145 types of tea, she and her colleagues rated green tea highest, with a blocking rate of 90 percent. Brick, Jasmine, oolong, and black tea followed in that order. They found that one gram of tea had some effect, and that three to five grams (three grams is one teaspoon) completely blocked the synthesis

---

Lu Yu, The Classic of Tea, translated by Frances Ross Carpenter

Tea is of the cold nature (meaning soothing) and may be used in case of blockage or stoppage of the bowels. . . . If one is generally moderate but is feeling hot or warm, given to melancholia, suffering from aching of the brain, smarting of the eyes, troubled in the four limbs, or afflicted in the hundred joints, he may take tea four or five times. Its liquor is like the sweetest dew of Heaven.

of nitrosamines in the human body. But it is too early to draw any conclusions, Dr. Han told the Beijing meeting.

Other research at Hamamatsu College found that green tea inhibits the action of MNNG (N-methyl-N1-nitro-N-nitrosoguanidine), a synthetic carcinogen. This substance decreased by 84 percent in the blood of mice drinking green tea and 82 percent with black tea. On mice fed Japanese green tea, induced malignant tumors did not develop as rapidly as in those not on tea, according to Oguni and other researchers at Shizuoka University's School of Pharmaceutical Science and the Hamamatsu College Department of Food Nutrition. Green tea also inhibits the action of aflatoxin, a powerful carcinogen produced by mold in stored crops such as grains and peanuts. This ability of tea to counteract this chemical has been demonstrated in several Chinese studies.

MAY PREVENT CELL MUTATION

Another way tea may help fight cancer is through preventing cell mutation. The antioxidation action of the polyphenols in green tea inhibit mutation of the DNA in healthy cells, which can cause them to become cancer cells. In rats injected with a cancer-causing substance and fed green tea, cancer did not develop, but it did in the control group without tea. This has been suggested by the findings of Cheng Shujin, Wang Zhiyuan, and Luo Huanzao, Cancer Research Institute, Academy of Chinese Traditional Medicine, Beijing; Professor Chi-tang Ho, Department of Food Sciences, Rutgers University Graduate School, and Huang Maoduan, Biological Research Institute, Roche Pharmaceutical Co., at the Symposium.

An antioxidant made from green tea applied to the skin significantly inhibited growth of induced skin cancer in mice. It is the EGCG catechin that improves fidelity of DNA replication, say Japanese researchers Tsuneo Koda and colleagues at Japan's National Institute of Genetics in "Detection and Chemical Identification of Natural Bio-Antimutagens, A Case of the Green Tea Factor," in *Mutation Research*

(Amsterdam, February 15, 1985).

In similar tests in Fujian province, green tea markedly decreased the incidence of lung cancer in rats (1.51 percent of the green tea drinkers developed it, and 3.38 of the non-tea control group). Jasmine and oolong tea were also tested, the former cutting cancer somewhat, but not as much as green tea. Oolong had no effect.

These researchers made the startling discovery that day-old green tea may help *produce* cancer. Rats drinking it had a higher rate of incidence than the control group which did not have tea. (Wu Suirong and others, Biochemistry Group, Fujian Traditional Medicine Research Institute, Fuzhou, at Symposium.)

BOOSTING IMMUNITY?

Those great polyphenols have also been found to increase white blood cells, the "soldiers" which fight infection in the human body. Tea extract is one of the main ingredients in a medicine now widely used with a high rate of success in China to counteract the reduction in white blood cells which accompanies radiation therapy. The medicine was developed by the Tea Research Institute in Hangzhou and other Chinese institutions.

In India too, researchers found that mice fed tea were less likely to develop leukemia when exposed to radiation.

A study of Jasmine tea by the Fujian Institute of Traditional Medicine and Pharmacology (Fujian is a big producer of Jasmine tea) found that tea heightened certain functions of the white blood cells in mice. In a related area, Soviet researchers say that tea helps the body excrete harmful radioactive strontium 90 before it settles in the bones. Chinese sources say tea can help absorb strontium 90 even after it has lodged in the bones. A mixture of black tea and the plant *viola inconspicua* achieved a 90 percent survival rate on animals subjected to intense radiation.

TEA AND YOUR HEART

Recent research indicates that tea may work against heart attacks, stroke, and thrombosis. Tea contributes to this in several ways. It does so in a general way through its role as gentle stimulant to the heart and circulatory system. Then, second, it strengthens and keeps the blood vessel walls soft. Third, there is evidence that the phenols in tea inhibit the absorption of cholesterol in the digestive tract, which could help decrease the cholesterol in the bloodstream. Fourth, it may decrease the blood's tendency to form thrombi, or unwanted clots. Often several of these functions operate together against stroke or heart attack. Strokes and thrombosis often occur because the blood vessels have lost their elasticity. Rutin has long been prescribed to keep these walls soft. One study found that feeding rabbits three percent oolong tea had nearly the same effect on the blood vessels as taking rutin. (Institute of Traditional Chinese Medicine and Pharmacology, Fuzhou, Fujian province.) In both China and other countries it was at one time believed that green tea contained a substance known as vitamin P which worked with vitamin C to strengthen the walls of the capillaries, the smallest blood vessels, preventing leakage of blood nutrients. A supplement called bioflavonoids, made from citrus rinds and with characteristics similar to flavanols or catechins, was popular among nutrition buffs. Later research concluded that it was not vitamin P performing this function, but something else, and the U.S. Food and Drug Administration prohibited the sale of bioflavonoids, saying they were worthless.

Something in tea, however, may still be the answer. Tea catechins were used with success in cases of hypertension to inhibit the action of an enzyme that constricts blood vessels. (Y. Hara, T. Matsuzaki, Food Research Laboratories, Mitsui Norin Co., Shizuoka, and T. Suzuki, Tokoku University, Sendai, Japan, at Symposium.)

Other tests by the Fuzhou researchers found that in patients with hypertension, coronary heart disease, atherosclerosis, or a high lipid level, drinking oolong tea (while taking no medicines) helped decrease blood viscosity, improve microcirculation, and prevent aggregation of blood platelets, which leads to unwanted clotting. Where thrombosis, or a clot, did occur, it took longer to form, and was of shorter duration.

TEA AGAINST CHOLESTEROL

Studies in several countries have found all three kinds of tea to have some effect in reducing cholesterol in blood fats, though oolong seems to get the best results. Triglycerides and cholesterol are the two important fat substances in the bloodstream. These are essential for many things, but cholesterol also builds up on the walls of the arteries, causing them to narrow and restrict blood flow, a condition known as atherosclerosis.

As far back as 1967 British researchers noted that black tea reduced cholesterol. Around 1980, tests in Japan indicated that regular drinking of oolong tea reduces cholesterol and neutral fats, and gives some help in cases of hypertension and coronary heart disease. (Haruo Nakamura, Jikei Research Laboratory, Japan.)

A University of California survey found less atherosclerosis among tea drinkers than coffee drinkers. This is borne out by findings at the Fujian institute mentioned above. Rabbits that drank oolong tea while on a high-cholesterol diet had smaller, more scattered, and less severe sclerosis spots on the aorta wall than the control group, which drank water.

Japanese researchers, testing with green tea, concluded that it is the catechins that act to cut cholesterol, and increase the excretion of total lipids and cholesterol in the feces. (K. Muramatsu, Food and Nutrition Laboratory, Department of Agricultural Chemistry, Faculty of Agriculture, Shizuoka University, and M. Fukuyo and Y. Hara, Mitsui Norin Co., Ltd., at the Hangzhou Symposium.)

Fibrinogen is a globulin in the blood which turns into fibrin to help in normal clotting. But in patients with abnormally high fibrinogen levels, fibrin joins with arterial wall cholesterol to form plaque. One catechin isolated from green tea helps dissolve fibrin. (Bao Jun and others at Zhejiang Medical College Second Affiliate Hospital, Hangzhou, at Symposium.) Six years of treatment with a medicine made from oxidized tea polyphenols on 214 cardiovascular patients with a high fibrinogen level brought it back to normal for 81 percent of them. (Xia Wuying, same hospital, at the Symposium.)

Poster from the Tea Association of China, Shanghai, sometime between 1907 and 1930. Both Chinese and British merchants stressed the healthful qualities of Chinese black tea to fight competition from Indian sellers.

An even better rate of 85 percent was reported on 120 high-fibrinogen patients given tea pigment (TP) as a medicine at another Zhejiang hospital. It can influence the anticoagulation enzyme, help dissolve fibrin, and also decrease the rate of aggregation of platelets and the adherence of platelets and cholesterol to the artery walls. (Luo Fuqing, Zhejiang Medical School Cardiovascular Research Institute, at the

---

L ong a matter of mystique in China for both age and extravagance of claims, Pu-erh, a dark-colored tea, (see p. 154) became the subject of study in several countries following a 1970s Chinese report on its effect in reducing blood fats. Articles about it as a "wonder drug" were inspired by European publication of findings at the Kunming Medical College First Hospital that Yunnan Tou Cha (Pu-erh molded in a bowl) lowered cholesterol levels 17 percent and triglycerides 22 percent. Investigations at the St. Antoine Hospital in Paris concluded that this tea did help reduce body weight and blood triglycerides and cholesterol.

A Free University of Berlin study in 1983, however, concluded that this tea had no clear effect, and another in France found that it acted only on triglycerides. But a study involving two universities and a medical center in Japan found that tea also reduced cholesterol, Pu-erh more effectively than green tea. And in Paris a month of three cups of Pu-erh a day brought lipids down 25 percent on 20 hyperlipidemia patients, while those on other teas showed no change. (Reported at a conference on this tea in Paris.) Meanwhile, researchers at Kunming Medical College claimed that Pu-erh was better than the commonly used medicine clofibrate, and had no side effects. Whether Pu-erh is truly more effective than other teas has not really been decided. Pu-erh is a rather unusual tea with some properties that others do not share. It will be fascinating to watch reports of further research to see whether these are a factor, and whether they, in turn, create any other problems.

Pu-erh—Cholesterol Special?

Symposium.) Professor Luo says that tea pigments are, with their anti-coagulant properties, abundant in both green and black tea.

Drinking of oolong tea itself for a month was reported to yield an 81 percent return to normal of high lipids in 424 patients at six big hospitals in the city of Guangzhou (Canton). (He Moli and others at the Tea Research Institute, Guangdong Institute of Agricultural Sciences and the Guangdong People's Hospital, at the Symposium.) But it should be pointed out that when results are so spectacular from one experiment, much more research must be done to confirm the validity of the investigation. It is still far too early to say with certainty that oolong has this lipid-reducing effect.

The above information indicates that regular drinking of tea (although on which kind of tea the verdict is not yet in) may play a role in controlling blood fats and preventing accumulation of cholesterol in the arteries. Initial studies and tests also indicate greater possibilities for utilizing medicines made from tea in treating related conditions. "Keep drinking tea and you may avoid some of the worst heart diseases," Professor Luo Fuqing is quoted as saying. ("What's in a Name," by Vijay Dudeja, *Tea and Coffee Journal*, January 1989.)

Poster of China Tea
Association, London, 1912.

A SLIMMING EFFECT?

After these reports on the effect tea has on fats in the bloodstream, Chinese claims that it actually helps reduce the amount of fat in the tissues may seem less extravagant. Oolong tea seems to get the most publicity here, although any tea can do some good. Chinese material cites numerous cases of persons who lost weight while regularly drinking two or three cups of oolong a day. Similar claims for Pu-erh are corroborated by Japanese research. (I. Tomila, M. Sano, Laboratory of Health Science, School of Pharmaceutical Sciences, Shizuoka University, Japan, at the Symposium.) Oolong mixed with other herbal ingredients is the basis for a number of teas marketed especially for slimming. One is The Well Known Tea, which contains oolong and 15 other ingredients. A Chinese ad for Slimming Tea claims that drinking it for three months can drop up to 15 pounds off your weight.

T he Drink is declared to be most wholesome, preserving in
perfect health until extreme Old Age.

Garway's Broadsheet,
London, 1660

LONGEVITY AND AGING

Long ago in China, tea was an ingredient in immortality potions favored
by the Taoists, who were keen on that subject. Still today, perhaps as an
echo of those beliefs, claims are made that tea drinking helps one to live
to a ripe old age. While it is no magic fountain of youth, some of its
benefits can be said to contribute to longevity (stimulation of bodily
functions, strengthening the immune system, reducing the chance of
heart disease and improving stomach functions). The fluoride in tea can
strengthen bones and help ward off osteoporosis in the same way that
it strengthens dental enamel. Investigation into whether tea has any
further effect on longevity and, if so, why, is only just beginning.

Chinese researchers found that 1 percent jasmine tea extended the life
of fruit flies to 40.5 days, more than double that of the control group,
which drank plain water and had a life span of 16.5 days. On a 5 percent
solution they lived 28.6 days. Oolong tea, in other tests, doubled the
lifespan. (Monographs by the Fujian Institute of Traditional Medicine,
Fuzhou, circulated by the Tea Branch of the Fujian provincial import/
export corporation.)

Thus far, it is not understood what compounds in tea could have this
effect on insects, and it would obviously require much additional
research to determine whether such reported effects of tea on the span
of insects' lives could be duplicated in an entirely different species.

Leaflet picked up in Cupertino,
California, for one of several
such teas.

FIGHTS TOOTH DECAY

Tea has turned out to be a double-barrelled threat to tooth decay for both the polyphenols (tannin) and the fluoride it contains. Polyphenols tend to reduce the formation of plaque, while fluoride strengthens tooth enamel so that it can resist decay. Some Chinese and American researchers have concluded independently that two or three cups a day, or, some say, only one of black tea, can decrease tooth decay.

The polyphenols bind themselves to mouth bacteria before the latter can form plaque, according to Dr. Laurence E. Wolinsky, associate professor of oral biology at the School of Dentistry of the University of California at Los Angeles. He found an exceptionally low rate of dental problems among people who drank a lot of tea.

A joint test in two other U.S. universities found that tea drinking "significantly inhibited" the growth of mouth bacteria. People who were tested with four different kinds of tea developed notably fewer cavities than those in a control group drinking plain water. The study, conducted at the Ohio State University College of Dentistry, Columbus, Ohio, and the Washington University School of Dental Medicine, St. Louis, Missouri, listed four teas sold under the names Young Hyson, Panfried, Lung Ching, and Chinese Green. Young Hyson and Panfried produced the best results. This was due, the report said, both to tannin and fluoride, probably more to the latter.

Chinese researchers say that the human body consumes from one to three milligrams of fluoride a day, which must be obtained from food and drink. Ten grams of tea leaves a day, enough for two cups of strong tea, will replace this, according to their calculations. Green tea contains twice as much fluoride as black, Dr. Sheldon Margen, professor of Public Health Nutrition at the University of California, wrote in the *U.C. Berkeley Wellness Newsletter.* Since the mid-1940s, fluoride has been added to drinking water in many communities in the United States and elsewhere. An analysis of the fluoride content of teas sold in the United States found a range of 1.32 to 4.18 parts per million (ppm), according to a U.S. study. Recommended fluoridation of water in the United States ranges from 0.7 ppm in warm areas, where more water is drunk, to 1.2 ppm. Therefore anyone who drinks two cups a day of the highest-ranking tea would get 8.36 ppm per day, just a little less than someone who drinks 8 glasses of fluoridated water, taking in 9.6 ppm. Three cups of tea with less than the highest fluoride content ought to do the trick. Chinese researchers found that loose Gunpowder tea (a green tea) contains 100–150 ppm, 60 to 80 percent of which can be extracted.

While fluoridation of water is obviously desirable because it also reaches children, who are not generally tea drinkers, the information above should be good news for people who live in areas without fluoridation, for by drinking tea they can derive the same benefit. For sensitive teeth, a twice-daily rinsing of the mouth with tea before swallowing it, if done over a long period of time, is said to be effective.

GERMICIDAL POTENTIAL?

Some researchers claim tea acts as a mild germicide in the digestive tract to help prevent food poisoning and diseases like cholera, typhoid, and dysentery. "The antibacterial effects of tea have been well documented in Chinese scientific literature," writes Dr. Albert Y. Leung in *Chinese Herbal Remedies.* "Green teas have stronger effects than black teas. They are effective against many types of bacteria, including those that cause dysentery, diphtheria, and cholera. . . . Tea in the form of a decoction was particularly effective . . . in treating bacillary dysentery, amoebic dysentery, acute gastroenteritis (inflammation of stomach and intestine), and enteritis (inflammation of the intestine)." There are reports of its use against plague bacilli in Japan.

Research on this point was sparked by an incident in a Taiwan restaurant in 1980. An entire table of diners, except for one man, got sick from eating contaminated shrimp. Curious as to why that person was missed, Professor E. Ryu of National Taiwan University investigated and concluded that it was because he was a heavy tea drinker. Then, in laboratory tests, Professor Ryu found that powdered tea added to agar plates of eight kinds of bacterial cultures (including those for dysentery, salmonella, cholera, staphylococcus) kept all but one from developing colonies of bacteria. Only the *E. coli* developed some, but fewer than usual. Another test produced similar results, this time also on streptococcus bacteria. Black, green and oolong tea had the same effect.

Tea drinking, particularly after a meal, is "a great contribution to the prevention of a variety of contagious diseases," Professor Ryu concluded. (*International Journal of Zoonoses*, no. 7, 1980, and, with Donald C. Blenden and David Wendall, no. 9, 1982.)

Cuts can benefit from washing in tea if there is nothing more medicinal around. Washing with tea is thought to prevent breaking out on the face. It is a treatment for athlete's foot, and dried used tea leaves in the socks prevent a recurrence. A home remedy for sunburn in the West is cold tea. Chewed tea leaves placed on insect bites are said to relieve the discomfort.

ANYTHING BAD ABOUT TEA?

We have mentioned above that because of the caffeine factor, over two cups a day is not recommended for pregnant women and nursing mothers. Persons with irregular heartbeats are advised to be cautious, as should those with stomach ulcers, for fear of stimulating too much stomach acid.

But does tea have any bad effects on healthy people? One thing that everyone should know is: never swallow medicines with tea. Some of the four hundred chemical compounds identified in it might cause an adverse reaction when combined with certain drugs.

British researchers have been concerned that tea growing in soil with high aluminum content will transmit levels of it harmful to people with aluminum-related problems. But this is a specific question related only to certain soils. Tea has some effect on solubility of iron and calcium, therefore on ease of absorption, a study at the University of Wisconsin found. While iron as a nutrient proved to be totally soluble in instant tea, solubility was only 85 percent in green and oolong tea and 69 percent in black. Research is being done on how to overcome this drawback. The Wisconsin study discovered that addition of the enzyme tannase, or lemon juice, increased iron solubility by 27 percent and that of calcium by 24 percent. There seems to be some point in putting lemon in black tea.

BY WAY OF SUMMARY

If one is to make anything at all of the above material, it must be that the time is just not ripe to draw any real conclusions as to what various teas are capable of, and which are best for you. However, on the basis of research thus far, some teas do stand out in certain respects. Here is a tentative summary of the claims made based on research to date:

Digestion	All kinds
Anti-bacterial	All kinds, but not fully confirmed
Cancer prevention	Green
Heart	Oolong and Pu-erh for cholesterol, green and oolong for blood vessels
Slimming	Oolong and Pu-erh
Tooth care	Green
Longevity/Anti-aging	All of the above; special emphasis on green for fluoride to combat osteoporeosis

(For another summary listing of the special benefits of certain teas according to Chinese tradition, see pp. 161–62.)

Whatever modern science finally concludes, the intuition and experience of ordinary people has certainly built tea a reputation as a health-giver over the centuries. The following story told by J. M. Scott in *The Great Tea Venture*, is a good example from recent times of how tea gains respect. In December 1941, as World War II began, forty thousand already exhausted refugees in Burma had to flee through the jungles of

Assam further south in India after the Japanese bombed their airlift field. The Indian tea growers' association was helping the refugees, so at least they had tea. Scott writes:

> The supply of food was a perpetual problem, and in any case, many of the refugees were in so advanced a state of starvation and exhaustion that a first real meal of solid food endangered their lives. But tea, being light, was always carried by the rescuers, and whenever a fire could be lit it was brewed. Alcohol, on the rare occasions when it was administered, proved a dangerous, even fatal stimulant. But hot, sweet tea saved lives again and again.

TEN *How to Make a "Nice Cup of Tea"*

T hese rules, combining the best of East and West, are in general
applicable to all kinds of tea—green, black, or oolong.

1. Use fresh cold water. Let the cold tap run for awhile first to avoid
   flat-tasting water (and also to avoid lead that may have dissolved
   into it while standing in the pipe). For this same reason, never make
   tea with water from the hot tap. (For more on water, see below.)
2. While the water is heating, get the tea things ready. A small pot is
   preferable to a large one, as the amount of boiling water used in a
   large one may "stew" the leaves and result in flat-tasting tea. Warm
   the pot (of pottery or other ceramic material) by rinsing it with hot
   water. If you wish, you can measure the rinse water in by cupfuls, so
   you will know just how far up to fill the pot when you actually make
   the tea. (This gauging won't be necessary after you become familiar
   with your teapot.)
3. Just before the water in the kettle boils, empty the teapot and add
   tea. For each cup use one teaspoonful of tea or one tea bag. For
   more than six cups, add an extra spoon "for the pot." If tea bags are
   used, they should be placed on the bottom of the pot so the water
   can hit them with full force.

   Some people use a perforated metal infuser or tea ball in a pot or
   mug, but connoisseurs frown on this, maintaining that the infuser
   prevents the water from fully saturating the leaves (this is also the
   criticism of tea bags, but their convenience may win out). If an

infuser is used, it should be no more than half full of leaves to allow room for them to expand.

4. Some people prefer water at a rolling boil. The air bubbles in it help spread out the tea leaves so that the water can get to them better. Others prefer it just before the full boil, when bubbles begin to rise, particularly for green tea. British wisdom teaches: Take the teapot to the water kettle, *never* the other way round—this applies to black tea, not green tea, which does not require as much heat.

   An optional step before adding boiling water to tea is called "rinsing the tea leaves." It is mandatory in making *gongfu* tea, but can improve any type except broken black tea. (Rinsing releases the compounds in the broken tea too rapidly, harming the flavor.) After the tea leaves have been added to the pot, pour in a little boiling water and drain it off immediately.

5. Finally, pour boiling water into the pot to the desired level and cover. British style is to keep the pot warm with a padded tea cosy, but the Chinese avoid this practice, feeling that it causes the leaves to stew, making them bitter and putting the chemical elements out of balance.

   If high-grade green tea is used, authorities from the Chinese Agricultural Institute advise leaving the lid off the pot, for these teas are easily stewed.

6. Let the tea stand. The best tea is made by *infusing* for a short time rather than *steeping* for a longer period. Three to five minutes is recommended, with the shorter time preferred. A kitchen timer is handy for this. Curled leaves take longer than flat ones and probably will need the full five minutes. Three is enough for most other teas. Very fine tea needs an extremely short time.

   Do not infuse any tea longer than five minutes, or it will become bitter. A longer time is not necessary, as the flavor and the tannin come out early in the infusion. A shorter time also reduces the caffeine. About three-fourths of the caffeine comes out in a five-minute infusion. Make time and not color your gauge of when the tea is ready, because color is not a good gauge of flavor. If you want stronger tea, use more leaves, not more time. The color comes out very quickly in black tea. Green tea should never get dark.

7. Rinse cups with hot water. If you use milk with black tea, now is the time to pour it into the cup. British tea drinkers swear by this. "Scalding" the milk with the hot tea gives it a particular desired flavor, they say. Another less poetic reason for putting milk in first is offered by none other than Samuel H. G. Twining, ninth generation of the family whose company supplies tea to the British crown: milk keeps the hot tea from cracking delicate porcelain cups. Never use cream. The tannin causes cream to curdle. Milk is never used with green tea, but sometimes with oolong.

8. Before pouring, stir the tea or shake the pot and then let the leaves settle. Pour into cups through a tea strainer. Green tea is of course taken without anything in it. If lemon and sugar are used with black tea, put the sugar in first, so it can dissolve well.

9. Strain off any tea left in the pot into another warmed pot, and cover with the tea cosy. Don't let the tea stand with the leaves in longer to make it darker.

10. The second infusion. Opinions differ on this according to the kind of tea and the authority. Many people say the second infusion is the best. In China, green tea drinkers start the day with some leaves in the bottom of their covered mugs and keep adding water before the cup is completely empty. Black and oolong teas can stand up through more infusions than green tea.

11. Never use tea that has stood overnight. Researchers at the Fujian province Chinese Medicine Research Institute found that while fresh green and oolong tea lowered incidence of lung cancer in rabbits, green tea that had stood overnight increased it.

ICED TEA

Use 50 percent more tea to allow for melting ice, the Tea Council of the USA recommends (three tea bags or spoonfuls for two glasses of iced

Making Tea. *Painting by Qi Baishi (1863–1957).*

tea). They give a recipe for two quarts:

> Bring one quart (4 cups) of water to boil in a saucepan. Remove from heat and add 15 tea bags or 1/3 cup loose tea. Stir, let stand five minutes. Keep at room temperature and pour over ice when ready to serve.

The Tea Council also offers a cold water method for a quart of "clear, cloudless iced tea":

> Soak 8 or 10 tea bags 6 hours or overnight in a quart of cold tap water (in room or refrigerator). Then remove the bags and squeeze them against the sides of the container. To serve, pour into ice-filled glasses.

No information is available on the chemical content of a glass of tea made this way. We prefer to sacrifice clear tea to safe tea and a guarantee of conventional flavor.

INSTANT TEA

Being instant is definitely this tea's advantage. The Tea Council advises following directions on the label, or in general, one level teaspoon instant tea to a teacup of boiling water, and 2 level tablespoons for each quart in a pot. For instant iced, 1 rounded teaspoon for a glass (6–8 ounces) of cold water or 2 rounded tablespoons for each quart of fresh cold water.

A WORD ABOUT TEA BAGS

Most real tea connoisseurs won't touch a tea bag, feeling it's not the Real Thing. The tea inside the tea bags does not consist of leaves but of the finest siftings, called "dust," so that the infusion is prompt. We find them expensive and wasteful, for they may produce tea that is either too strong or too much, and keeping a tea bag around for reuse is a messy business. Fine tea goes further when you can control exactly how much you use.

However, tea bags *are* convenient. Almost every kind of tea, including most Chinese varieties, is available in bags.

A FURTHER WORD ON WATER

The quality of water will affect the way the tea leaf components dissolve into the beverage, and therefore its quality. Lu Yu said spring water was best, followed by river water, and then well water. The amount of minerals in the water seems to have been a consideration. The problem is that nowadays it's practically impossible to find such "natural" water that is unpolluted, and tap water is frequently highly chlorinated. Various types of bottled spring water, now available everywhere, can yield satisfactory results. We recommend experimenting to find the best water.

WEIGHTS AND MEASURES

Three grams, or one teaspoonful, is the usual amount of dry leaves per cup. Both Chinese and American sources agree that a pound of tea makes about 200 cups. An ounce of instant makes 40 servings.

The floating world within a tea glass.

ELEVEN 🍃 *Judging, Storing, Other Uses*

How do you know whether you're getting good tea? It's hard if you buy it ready packaged. Then you'll have to learn by trial and error. It's easier when you can see your tea and buy it loose, as it is sold in some shops. The four criteria for good tea are appearance, color, aroma, and flavor. Here are a few guidelines, but individual teas provide many exceptions, as you will see in chapter twelve.

Appearance. Quality green tea should be clean and taut with leaf and bud in one piece. Such leaf sets also indicate that the leaves are young and tender therefore more flavorful. Quality runs in a descending order from bud/one leaf, bud/two leaves, and so on. Teas with incomplete leaves and bits are inferior quality. Exceptions are blends, which are composed of more than one kind of tea, broken black, and of course compressed teas.

Color. Quality tea leaves are glossy rather than dull. A properly made infusion should be clear, and with clear, bright color as a rule, reddish for black tea, yellowish green for green tea, a lively orange-brown to dark brown for oolong. Pu-erh is darker. Quality tea never produces a dull or muddy liquid.

Aroma. Oolong and black tea, because they are fermented, have more aroma than ordinary green unscented tea. There are many variations and exceptions.

Flavor. Fine tea should have a smooth, fresh taste. For green tea it should be fresh and light, and for black, stronger. Any hint of sharpness indicates that there is an imbalance of the tea's components. Bitterness

Tea tasters, Anxi.

is from excessive caffeine, over-sweetness from rich amino acids, harshness from tannins. Exceptions to the fresh taste rule are Pu-erh and other compressed teas, and Liubao.

The best tea comes from the early spring picking. The Chinese names frequently let you know this. Names denoting picking times are: spring tea: Chunfen, Qingming, and Guyu; summer tea: Lixia and Mangzhong; autumn tea: Liqiu and Bailu. For explanation of terms, see Solar Calendar on p. 173. Green tea should be used within a year after harvesting.

Teas directly from China are sold packaged under a number of brand names, in addition to the name of the specific tea. For a list, see p. 165. Other teas sold under major company labels may also be Chinese or a mixture of teas from China and other countries. Several big packers, including Twinings, Lipton, First Colony, and Grace, have their own lines of Chinese teas.

It is often wiser to buy a somewhat more expensive grade than the cheapest grade, for with the latter you may have to use a lot of tea and still may not get good flavor. Since a pound of tea makes at least 200 cups, even the most expensive tea is a low-priced beverage.

WHERE TO GET ALL THE TEA IN CHINA

If we have succeeded in sparking your interest in tea and its history, you may wonder where you can purchase or taste some of the teas described here. In Chapter Twelve we explain that not all will be available outside China, but some may be. We advise experimenting. The big American and British companies have lines that includes most of the familiar black teas. To get the full range you may have better luck in a speciality store than in your local supermarket.

A list of mail order sellers appears in Andrea Israel's 1987 book *Taking Tea*. In our own locality we found an excellent selection of several hundred teas, including a few unusual Chinese ones such as White Tea and Lichee Black, at Lisa's Tea Treasures (1203 Lincoln Avenue, San José, California 95125). Tea may be ordered by mail from this location.

The shop has an amazing collection of tea things, mostly Victorian, and serves special teas. Similar shops may be springing up in your area as well. Explore. Ten Ren (949 Grant Ave., San Francisco, California 94108) handles catalog orders over $10 of some Chinese teas, with emphasis on those from Taiwan. For teas imported from mainland China, a reliable mail order and retail source is Native Produce Co., 622 Broadway, San Francisco, California 94133.

For tea served in Japanese style and Japanese tea snacks, we discovered Daruma Foods (1290 Sixth Street, Berkeley, California 94710), which also handles mail orders for a number of Chinese teas.

HOW TO STORE

Tea must be kept dry. The best container is a metal box with a double lid, or a glass bottle with a tight cover. Better yet, one that is lightproof. In a store, loose tea keeps better than that packed in tins or boxes because it has a larger bulk. Some tea comes wrapped in tinfoil and boxed. If you expect to use it all in a month or two, it is all right to leave it in the original bag. Oolong tea (with 2–3 percent moisture compared to 5–7 percent in others) keeps longer. If tea gets damp you can spread it out in a pan and dry it in the oven.

Store tea in a cool, dry place, preferably well-ventilated. Tea absorbs other odors easily, so never keep it in a closet with mothballs or other strong-smelling substances. Once tea is tainted by an outside odor, it cannot be salvaged. One Guangdong tea shop owner is so particular about odors that he will not allow his employees to eat scallions or wear perfume in his establishment.

OTHER USES

Tea has many uses beyond that of a beverage. A popular way of eating eggs in China is to crack them slightly after boiling very briefly and boil them in a pot of leftover or fresh tea. This is well known as "tea egg." Tea leaves are also used in some styles of Chinese cooking, particularly that from Hangzhou in the tea country. They add a new and delicate flavor to familiar meat and fish dishes.

Tea is used as a gargle for fresh breath. Used or dry leaves are chewed to remove the odor of onions or garlic.

The Tea Research Institute in Hangzhou has found a way to extract a natural antioxidant from tea leaves. It is particularly welcomed in the mooncake business. Mooncakes with rich fillings of ham, black bean paste, coconut, sugar, or nuts are in great demand for the Mid-Autumn Festival (the Moon Festival) which usually falls in September. China's entire one billion people want their mooncakes at the same time, but when these delicacies are made too far in advance there is a risk of spoilage. The antioxidant seems to do the trick. Furthermore, it can be made from the low-quality leaves which are usually discarded.

From tea seeds, previously thrown away, the Institute has extracted an oil said to be superior to rapeseed oil, which is commonly used in stir-frying. Also extracted is a surface activator which improves the quality of foam construction bricks, and is an ingredient in a new type of shampoo.

TWELVE *🍃 Fifty Famous Chinese Teas*

I n this chapter we offer a choice of fifty teas to drink for your pleasure and health. Most are extremely well known in China. Many are not available for sale in the United States at present, and for others there is no reliable supply. However, visitors to China, particularly if they are near the area of production, are quite likely to encounter some of these teas, which may become more widely available in the future. The ones we have chosen are very famous, or have a colorful history or lore, an interesting process, or are otherwise distinguished. Many other teas are mentioned in passing.

A NOTE ON NAMES

We have listed teas both by their Chinese characters and by the names under which they are commmonly sold on the international market, rather than in strict conformity with the present-day Chinese pinyin romanization system of spelling. (For the pinyin equivalents, see p. 175.) When we have no evidence of the market name of a tea, we have used pinyin. So the spelling system of the names will necessarily appear inconsistent. Tea terms originated in many ways: from several languages, from commercial usage at various times, and from numerous authorities, so it is not surprising that there should be variations.

If you do not know Chinese, the Chinese characters can help avoid confusion about names if you are in a Chinese store because you can show the vendor the character in this book.

A tea may be sold boxed with simply its name (oolong, Lung Ching), or sold with the name and a brand name (for instance, Golden Sail Yingteh Black). The main brands packed in China are Temple of Heaven, Sprouting, Golden Sail, Sunflower, Peacock, Palace, Dragon, Evergreen, and Qing.

GREEN TEAS

In addition to the special kinds listed below, teas are marketed under the name China Green, or bear the name of the province, for instance Fujian Green, Guangxi Green (Guiqing). This does not necessarily indicate that they are an inferior grade of tea, and in fact some sold this way may be quite as good or identical with some of the "name brands" below. Unfortunately, quality may not be consistent due to the differences in picking times.

Why Teas Have So Many Names

Tea names came to the market from Fukienese (spoken in the southern province of Fujian), Cantonese (the southern province of Guangdong), from bastardized English pronunciation of these two and also of standard Chinese, which is based on the speech of the north. Most names became known by a romanization of one of these. Still today the Cantonese have their own names for every tea, and spelling based on variants of their pronunciation. Each province markets its teas under its own spelling, it seems. Thus Shoumei (Longevity Eyebrow) also comes out Sowmee in one area and Show Mee in another.

Chinese has been widely known abroad in the Wade-Giles romanization standardized by British diplomat Sir Thomas Wade in 1859 and modified by sinologist Herbert A. Giles in 1892. This did systematize things, but also led to mispronunciation by people who depended solely on it. Many tea names on the market today are in that

Chunmee (Chun Mei, Zhenmei) and Wuyuan Mingmei "Eyebrow" Teas

The shape of their processed leaves gives this name to Chunmee (Precious Eyebrow) and several other famous "eyebrow" teas. The beverage this tea produces has a distinct plumlike flavor, and has long been popular abroad.

The plum seems to be prominent in the minds of the tea growers of northeastern Jiangxi province's Wuyuan county, for when they began producing a new high-quality green tea in 1950, they called it Mingmei (Famous Plum). It has lived up to its name for fame.

Mingmei is produced from Shangmeizhou (Upper Plum Islet), a fine tea strain whose fat, hairy buds usually emerge quite late. Great skill is used in the second wok firing to achieve the right shape. Temperature, length of time, and hand movements must be well coordinated. The fine, taut, jade green, eyebrow-shaped leaves have been likened to a work of art. The clear, yellowish green beverage has a mellow flavor. Mingmei is also used as a base for scented teas.

---

spelling, for instance Lung Ching (Longjing in pinyin).

A single tea may be known by several names, even in Chinese. These could include its chief name and another which it may have picked up in history, such as Imperial Tribute. Or it may be known by its chief name preceded by one or several geographical additions (province, district, county, locality, nearby mountain or river), any of which might be used some of the time.

Even if it has only one name (let us say for simplicity), a single tea could still have as many as eight designations—with those for possibly four grades, four pickings, and combinations thereof. (Names of seasonal pickings are given on p. 173–4.)

Names have changed over the centuries. Bohea (already a variant of Wuyi, the name of a mountainous tea-growing area in Fujian province), originally meant in England a high-grade black tea from Fujian, later a much lesser grade, and now is rarely used. The names

Not far west of Wuyuan county lies the famous porcelain center, Jingdezhen, which has provided so many beautiful tea things (see pp. 68–69).

Dafang Tea, Famous for Scenting

The Huangshan Mountains in southeastern Anhui province where this tea is grown are among China's best-known scenic spots. They are famous for their "four uniques"—high, steep, unusual-shaped peaks; grotesquely shaped ancient pines; clear, trickling springs; and surging

---

of some large areas were once synonymous with a kind of tea, but in these places many smaller units may now exist, each marketing tea under its own name.

Historically, Chinese tea production and the international tea trade, largely British, proceeded each in its own direction, paying little regard to the other's language. Then, too, Chinese tea merchants, or their translators, were more interested in selling than in spelling—in any language. And most English-speaking people who write about tea don't know Chinese. All these factors added to the confusion. American tea merchants ignore most names and order by number.

In 1978 the Chinese government adopted the pinyin form of phonetic spelling which more accurately represents *putonghua* (the "common speech," sometimes called "Mandarin" outside China), which is the standard national language based on the pronunciation of the north. This spelling is now used by the United Nations, and the *New York Times* and other major publications. Some Chinese tea companies market their products in the pinyin spelling, but many are understandably reluctant to change a name already known throughout the world. Oolong, for example, in pinyin would be *wulong* (black dragon). But oolong is so well known that it even appears in English-language dictionaries, so oolong it remains.

seas of clouds. These cloud seas create a perfect natural environment for growing tea and indeed this is the home of many famous teas—Tunlu (see p. 141) and Taiping Houkui (see p. 139) among the greens, and Keemun Black (see p.147).

Another Huangshan tea is Dafang, with leaves flat like those of the more famous Lung Ching, but rougher. After processing they are yellowish brown in color. The beverage is a pale yellow and has a strong chestnut flavor. This tea comes from Shexian county in the Huangshan Mountains.

Scented with jasmine or magnolia blossoms, Dafang becomes Huadafang (Flower Dafang), a famous scented variety.

E Ruizi (Emei Ruizi), from a Sacred Mountain

Mt. Emei in Sichuan province is one of China's four mountains sacred to Buddhism. Many secular travelers also visit it to tour the historic temples and enjoy the green wooded scenery. Another of the joys of the mountain for some is to drink E Ruizi tea, which is only available in China. The mountain mists make many areas around Mt. Emei famous tea producers.

E of course means Mt. Emei, and Ruizi means "pistils." The buds of the processed tea look like pistils among the dark green eyebrow-shaped leaves covered with fine hair.

This tea is known for its lift to the spirits, and the feeling of relaxation it imparts. Picking takes place about ten days before Qingming Festival (early April) when the buds are the size of a grain of rice. The beverage is a clear green with a strong aroma and long-lasting aftertaste.

Gunpowder, Pingshui Gunpowder (Zhucha)

Legend has it that the name Gunpowder was given by a young English clerk in the tea trade who thought its tiny, tightly rolled green balls looked like gunpowder. It was formerly sold in sizes with identifications like Pinhead and Pea Leaf. The Chinese name Zhucha (Pearl Tea) is also an apt description. Pingshui refers to the town of Pingshui lying southwest of Shanghai across Hangzhou Bay, or more specifically, south

of Shaoxing in Zhejiang province. Gunpowder is produced there and in surrounding counties.

Rolling the choice tender leaves into this unusual shape requires special skill. But—good news—these tightly rolled nuggets have the ability to keep longer than other green teas, which quickly lose their flavor in storage.

When tea is made, the tiny pellets jingle and tinkle into the pot or cup. Boiling water causes them to open up like flowers and float or sink slowly to the bottom in graceful patterns of dark and lighter greens which add a dimension of visual pleasure to tea drinking. They produce a strong, dark-green brew with a memorable fragrance, a slightly bitter but not unpleasant flavor, and a long-lasting aftertaste. Gunpowder is heavier than most other teas, so three to five grams (one to two teaspoons) to a pot is the recommended amount.

Chinese exporters also recommend Gunpowder for iced tea flavored with lemon and sugar, though they probably do not drink it themselves, as tea is always served hot in China. Gunpowder is popular in Morocco, where the leaves are boiled and mint and sugar are added.

Gunpowder was one of the first Chinese teas to be exported, beginning in the early seventeenth century. When it was presented as tribute to Emperor Kang Xi (r. 1661–1722), it became one of his favorites. In the early eighteenth century, despite its relatively high price, this tea enjoyed popularity in Europe under the names Green Pearl and Hyson. The latter came from the Chinese Xi Chun, meaning (Kang) Xi Spring. The name Hyson later became associated with a completely different long, twisted tea.

China's highest historical point in Gunpowder production was in the decade 1883–1894. It was once very popular in the United States, comprising nearly two-thirds of all tea imported there in 1860. Today China's exports far surpass that historical high, and the price has been made lower by volume production.

In 1984 Temple of Heaven Brand Special Gunpowder won a gold medal at the Twenty-third Judging of the International Institute for Quality Selections in the Canned Food and Other Food Products Selection held in Madrid. The Institute is composed of members from ten countries in Europe and the Americas.

Gunpowder tea is held to be high in fluoride, known to reduce dental caries—100 to 150 parts per million, 60 to 80 percent of which can be extracted, according to Chinese researchers. They say the human body uses 1–2 milligrams of fluoride a day, which must be obtained from food and drink. Ten grams of Gunpowder (enough for two strong cups) can supply this amount.

Huading Yunwu (Huading or Tiantai Cloud and Mist)

This is one of several "cloud and mist" teas grown in different provinces. Huading is the highest of all the peaks of Mt. Tiantai in eastern Zhejiang province, and connoisseurs rank this aromatic yellow-green beverage in the higher class of "cloud and mist" teas. It is also known as Tiantai Yunwu. Under the name Tiantai Special Grade, this tea won international prizes in 1984 and 1986, a gold laurel in Paris and another gold metal for quality in Geneva.

This area has clouds and mist the year round, but would normally not be considered good tea country because of the strong winds on the peak and severe winter cold. The tea growers have overcome these obstacles by planting windbreaks. The leaves are fired twice, once before rolling and a second time afterward.

Huangshan Mao Feng (Huangshan Hairpoint)

While not strictly a scented tea, this variety produces an apricot-colored beverage with the fragrance of magnolias, even though none grow nearby. Perhaps the wild peach trees blossoming all over the hills surrounding Huangshan in Anhui province make some contribution. And perhaps that is why one authority lists it among the five best known teas in China. Huangshan tea drinkers have a saying: the first cup is most fragrant, the second sweetest, the third, strongest.

Plucked very young at the stage of only a bud and a single unfolding leaf, the leaves when processed are yellowish green, flat with a very slight upturn, and covered with silvery hair. The Qingming (early April) picking is sold as a special choice grade.

Every part of the Chinese countryside has its legends which reflect the tragedy of life of old China, and there is one linked with Huangshan

Mao Feng. A young man and a beautiful young woman from a tea plantation were in love, but the local tyrant seized her for his concubine. She escaped, only to learn that the landlord had killed her lover. When she found the lover's body deep in the mountains, she wept and wept, until she became the rain, while her lover's body turned into a tea bush. That is why, says the legend, the area where this tea grows is cloudy and humid the year round.

Huiming, from Tang Times

It is said that this tea was drunk as early as the Tang dynasty, but that it only became popular in the Qing dynasty. In the twentieth century it gained international repute by winning a first-grade certificate at the 1915 Panama Pacific International Exposition held in San Francisco to celebrate the completion of the Panama Canal. The plant is a broad-leafed strain with many small buds, which can still be seen after it is processed. The beverage has a mellow taste and long-lasting flower flavor.

Huiming Temple, which gives this tea its name, stands halfway up a peak called Mt. Chimu in southern Zhejiang province. The tea grows on the slopes around it, which are generally within the level of almost perpetual mist and cloud.

Jingting Luxue (Jingting Green Snow)

A small snowstorm among the swirling green leaves in the cup is created by the prominent white hairs on the leaves of this tea, hence the name.

Old books describe it as one of the famous tribute teas presented to the emperors as early as the Eastern Jin dynasty (A.D. 317–420) and on up through Ming and Qing. If this information is reliable, it dates the beginning of tribute tea much earlier than the usually accepted time during the reign of Emperor Tang Tai Zong (626–649). However, the word generally translated as "tribute," a euphemism for a form of taxation, is often used rather loosely to mean "gift."

This rather rare tea is not available abroad or indeed in many parts of China. It is sold only near the place where it is grown, Mt. Jingting in eastern Anhui province. But if you ever find yourself near the cities of Suzhou or Zhenjiang in nearby Jiangsu province, you must sample its fresh, aromatic taste, and might want to take some home.

Jiukeng, from Wild Trees

Wild tea trees provide the leaves, or most of them anyway, for this famous tribute variety of the Tang dynasty. They grow in small clumps all about the hills and valleys of Jiukeng township in Chun'an county in west central Zhejiang province.

Once in spring and again in summer the people go out for the plucking. From trees standing about as tall as a man they remove the branches and usable parts and carry them home. There the thick, fat, glossy yellow-green leaves are stripped off.

The processed leaves are sold under several different names:

> Maojian (Hair Point) plucked before Qingming in early April, the best and most famous, and the basis of some high-grade scented teas.
>
> Yuqian (Pre-Rain—the Grain Rain, April 20)

Three made from the crop after that rain are:

> Hongqing (de-enzymized by baking)
>
> Chaoqing (de-enzymized by panfiring)
>
> Hongchaoqing (de-enzymizd by both processes)

The latter three kinds became known abroad under different names, as formerly the crude tea was sold to local tea factories which packaged and sold it under the names Chun Mei, Feng Mei, Emei, Hyson (Xi Chun, see Hyson entry in Glossary), Song Luo, and Xiumei.

Teas from Chun'an and the former Suian county nearby are often sold together under the name Suilu (Sui Green). With flower fragances added, the first picking (see above) is sold as Huamaojian (Flower Maojian), Huayuqian (Flower Pre-rain), both favorites in north China.

Kooloo (Gulao), an Ancient Tea

This tea is said to have been drunk for l500 years, which would date it to the sixth century. It is named for the town of Gulao (meaning very old) southwest of Guangzhou in Guangdong province.

Everything about this unusual green tea suggests its ancient origin—its brew of bright brownish red color, its slightly burnt flavor with a sweet aftertaste. It is available on the market in China but, carried abroad by people from Guangdong, is more popular in Hongkong, Macao, and Australia.

Gulao Town is located in the Pearl River delta southwest of Guangzhou. There, in a low area between two mountains, the weather is warm and misty the year round—fine for tea growing.

After the leaves are plucked they are made into crude tea in the usual way through sun drying, firing, and rolling. Then they are given ten turns in a rolling drum heated to about 570 Fahrenheit (300 degrees centigrade). It's a tricky business to impart its burnt taste without scorching the leaves. They are done when they can be easily kneaded into a powder.

Lanxi Maofeng (Lanxi Hairpoint)

This is a relatively new green tea created only in 1973. One special thing about it is that at the time of plucking, the sprouts of this strain are longer than the just-unfolding leaves. This is one reason for its flavorful infusion. Leaves and bud must also stay together. When processed, the former become stout strips covered with silvery hair that yield a clear yellow-green tea with a mellow, slightly sweet taste.

Lanxi Maofeng is produced in the misty mountains cut up by tributaries of the Fuchun River in northern and western Lanxi county in central Zhejiang province. The best of several teas produced there is that from Yezhu Tan. It is one of the Panshan or west county teas.

While Maofeng is a quality tea in its own right, it is often scented to produce Jinhua Moli Maofeng (Jinhua Jasmine Hairpoint). Jinhua is the name of the prefecture. This tea is well liked both in China and abroad.

Lingyun White Down (Baihao)

A wild tea tree whose buds and leaves are covered with white down—held to greatly enhance the flavor—is native to hilly Lingyun county in the western part of the Guangxi Zhuang autonomous region. In its natural state the tree grows to a height of twenty to thirty feet. The local people have cultivated a dwarf variety which keeps the original characteristics but is easier to care for.

The leaves, needle-shaped when rolled, produce a bright green tea with a sweet, mellow taste and a lingering fragrance remininscent of chestnuts.

Liuxi Tea, Aid to Digestion

Liuxi green tea is prized around the city of Guangzhou for its benefits to the digestive system, but is not widely known abroad. It is included here specifically for its health factor.

Users say Liuxi from the spring harvest is exceptionally good for keeping bowel movements regular and for treating constipation and digestive disorders. It is more astringent than ordinary green tea, and believed to be more effective at alleviating discomfort after a heavy meal. The used leaves of the early spring tea are also eaten as an aid to digestion, and in the belief that their sweet aftertaste is soothing to the throat. It has also been credited with dissolving kidney stones.

No scientific conelusions on its healing powers have been reached, but some Hongkong residents make a special trip to the tea-growing area or Guangzhou (Canton) once a year to lay in a supply of the spring crop.

Grown on mountain terraces on the upper reaches of the Liuxi (Flowing Stream) River in Conghua county north of Guangzhou, this tea is produced from either the large-leaved Yunnan variety or Baimao (White Hair), a local strain. The trees reach a height of about four feet.

The processed leaves are in the form of rough, dark green strips. They produce a light brownish-orange beverage with a sweet aftertaste. For a more flavorful drink or just a change of taste, we recommend mixing leaves of this tea with those of oolong.

In the Chinese medical view, Liuxi alleviates heat, and therefore is in the "cool" category. Users are advised to keep this aspect in mind if it is to be drunk daily in large quantities, and compensate by using less tea per infusion, or eating more nutritious food.

Lu'an Guapian (Lu'an Melon Seeds)

Perhaps the unusual appearance of this tea has contributed to its position as one of the five best-known green teas inside China. The processed leaves are shaped like melon seeds. This is a product of Lu'an county in the Dabie Mountains of western Anhui province.

Instead of plucking two leaves and a bud as is customary for most teas, the farmers have traditionally preferred to break off sections of the branches (in a controlled way, let us hope) and separate the leaves and buds at home. From the buds they make other varieties of high-quality tea: Yinzhen (Silver Needles, made from the buds); from the first leaf, Tipian (Emerging Plates); from the second leaf, Guapian; and from the third, Meipian (Plum Blossom Petals).

A special step in processing Guapian is heat-drying over alternately low and high heat. This helps form the shape and adds to the strong, fresh aroma of a sweet beverage with a long-lasting infusion.

Lung Ching (Longjing, Dragon Well), the Cooling Tea

Since mentioned by Lu Yu himself, Lung Ching tea, one of China's most famous, has been celebrated in prose and poem, including works by famed Tang poet Su Dongpo. It is known for "four uniques": its green color, mellow taste, aroma, and beautiful shape. It is considered to have a cooling effect and is frequently served in hot weather.

The flat, green leaves produce a clear, yellow-green tea with a slightly sweet, aromatic earthy flavor and a lingering aftertaste which is one of this tea's particular characteristics.

Lung Ching means Dragon Well (the dragon is the king of the waters in Chinese mythology). The home of this tea is the village of that name west of the famed West Lake in Zhejiang province, which lies southwest of Shanghai. Another growing area southwest of the lake is known as Nine Crooks and Eighteen Gullies (Jiuqu Shibajian), which includes Meijia Village and Lion Peak. At Lion Peak, Qing dynasty Emperor Qian Long drank this tea at the Wugong Temple. So pleased was he that he conferred the title Imperial Tea on the produce of the eighteen tea trees growing outside the temple.

Lung Ching has indeed some unique and wonderful features. The finest grade, Qiqiang (Flagged Spear) Lung Ching has a bud and only one leaf, thus being younger and superior to the customary "two leaves and a bud" tea. In the cup, the buds float in the water with the leaves pointing upright like spears, hence the name. The next grade, with two leaves, is known as Queshe (Sparrow's Tongue) Lung Ching.

A pound of dry Lung Ching contains 25,000 bud-and-leaf sets, each snipped off individually by skilled fingers. Lung Ching, unlike other teas, is not rolled to shape the leaves. Pan-frying the leaves requires great skill to match the temperature to the tenderness of the leaves. Lung Ching tea won the Gold Medal with Palms at the 1988 meeting of the International Institute for Quality Selection.

The best infusion of Lung Ching is made with water from Hupao (Tiger Run) Spring, one of four nearby famous for their clear, sweet water. This is a fault area of the Tiyun Mountains, with plenty of quartzite rock which provides good filtration for the spring water. Visitors to Hangzhou are almost always taken to Hupao Spring for a cup of Lung Ching tea.

Lushan Yunwu Tea (Lushan Cloud and Mist)

An old saying claims this tea increases longevity. The same mountains that make Mt. Lushan one of the most beautiful peaks in China, and a celebrated resort, make the area good tea country. Lushan is located in Jiangxi province in a cleft between the Yangtze River and Lake Poyang, both of which help provide water for the mist and clouds that wreathe its peaks.

Here is where the Tea Sage Lu Yu wrote his famous book, which mentions Lushan Yunwu tea. About it the Tang dynasty poet Bai Juyi wrote:

> Emerald tea trees on Lushan
> Are hidden in swirling mist.
> Light spring breezes waft perfume.
> No wine can touch the senses
> Like this tea made with spring water.

The plant from which this tea comes has stout, thick leaves covered with fine white down. The shrub was grown as early as the Tang dynasty. By the Song dynasty an excellent species had been developed and around A.D. 1000 its product became an imperial tribute. The beverage has a sweet taste and refreshing fragrance. This tea is rated among China's top ten.

Mengding Tea, an Early Prescription

A story about this tea illustrates the very early use of the beverage as a medicine. In the late Western Han dynasty (206 B.C.–A.D. 24) the Buddhist monk Pu Hui planted seven tea trees in a temple garden on Mt. Menghan, which stands on the western edge of Sichuan's Chengdu Plain. Tea from these trees was believed to cure illnesses and prolong life, so was known as Tea of the Immortals (*Xian Cha*). All other tea from the area was merely referred to as "the other (meaning "earthly") kind." To this day, the tea is called "Number One Under Heaven." Mengding means "Meng summit." Historical records say that most of the early tea grown in Sichuan came from Mengding.

From the mid-Tang dynasty to mid-Qing, Mengding Green was a tribute tea. In early spring the county magistrate would lead the monks and local populace out to pick the choice young buds and leaves from these trees. After processing, the product was rushed to the emperor for use in ceremonial offerings. It became known by the name Main Tribute.

This tea is also known as Thunderclap, from this story: An elderly monk living near one of the tea gardens always felt cold and doctors could find no cure. The manager of the garden came to see him and told him about this Thunderclap tea. At the first thunderclap of the second lunar month (March), he told the monk, go out and pick some tea on the central peak.

One ounce, he said, would cure the illness, two would keep him healthy for the rest of his life, three would change his very bones, four would make him immortal. The monk, able to gather only one ounce, recovered, but did not gain immortality.

Mengding tea used to be produced in very small quantities. Only ninety leaves a year were plucked by the monk who maintained the trees, according to a Qing dynasty source. Now it is more widely grown in the area. The various local products have fanciful names: Sweet Dew (Ganlu), Stoneflower (Shiya), Yellow Sprout (Huangya), for the best kinds. There are also Everlasting Spring Silverleaf (Wanchun Yinye) and Rice Sprout (Miya). Stoneflower and Yellow Sprout produce a yellowish tea, while that from the others is green.

In order to differentiate these products from those of other places, they are prefixed by the name Mengding. The name means "misty peak," and the three "mosts" for which the mountain is known—rain, mist, and clouds—contribute to this tea's excellence. Some hold it to be Sichuan's best.

Pi Lo Chun (Biluochun, Green Snail Spring)

For centuries this very famous aromatic light green tea was known by the name Xia Sha Ren Xiang (Astounding Fragrance). A legend explains why. Once in the distant past, some pickers of a particularly good crop filled their baskets before they were ready to go home. Wanting to carry more leaves, they stuffed the excess inside their tunics. Warmed by body heat, the leaves began to give off a rich aroma. "I was astounded," many pickers said, and the name stuck.

Sometime in the late seventeenth or early eighteenth century Emperor Kang Xi visited the Lake Taihu area in Zhejiang province and was presented with this tea. He liked it, but said the name was too vulgar, and suggested a new name, Pi Lo Chun, Green Snail Spring. The processed leaves, tightly rolled in spiral shape, do look like tiny green snails.

The name is now known all over the world, for this is one of China's famous rare teas. Its home is two mountains known as East and West

Dongting which poke up out of Taihu, the great lake not far west of Shanghai, and where the garden city of Suzhou is located. One mountain is an island in the lake and the other a peninsula. The water evaporating from the lake keeps them overhung with clouds and mist, thus the young leaves stay moist.

A further attraction is the fact that between the tea bushes are planted peach, plum, and apricot trees. They are in full bloom just as the unfolding tea leaves are at their tenderest and most receptive to absorbing the fragrance of the blossoms. This gives Pi Lo Chun tea a unique aroma and clean flavor.

Plucking time begins at the spring equinox and reaches its height early in April. After that time leaves are no longer at their prime. Plucking takes only the bud and a single leaf half unfurled, called the "sparrow's tongue." The leaf is full of fine white hairs. A mere pound of it contains sixty to seventy thousand leaf-bud sets. Processing is done by hand, and it takes great skill, for if the rolling of the roasting leaves is not carefully done, they will not achieve their perfect snail shape.

Putuo Fo Cha (Putuo Buddhist Tea)

Mt. Putuo, rising like a mirage out of the sea, is one of the three hundred islands of the Zhoushan Archipelago just outside the Yangtze estuary. It is a famous Buddhist retreat and one of China's four mountains sacred to that faith. Legend has it that the bodhisattva Guanyin meditated and preached there before attaining enlightenment.

The island and its three hundred temples are maintained chiefly by monks, who grow fruit and other produce for sale to help support themselves. Their tea bushes provide Puto Fo Cha, held to be one of the five most famous in China. Served to guests, it is sold only on the island, and is highly prized as a souvenir gift. It is reputed to be a remedy for diarrhea and lung lesions. The great Ming dynasty pharmacologist Li Shizhen wrote in his *Canon of Medicinal Herbs* that it was used to treat hemorrhages and dysentery.

The glossy green finished leaves are tadpole shaped, neither round nor in strips, and the clear beverage has a fresh aroma.

Qiangang Huibai (Qiangang Brilliant White), a Rare Tea

The farmers in Qiangang village used to make this tea just for themselves, and reserve some for gifts for special friends. Now, however, more is available for sale and Qiangang has become one of the most valued green teas in China. It is available at present in large cities of the Yangtze valley, such as Shanghai, Nanjing, Hangzhou, and Suzhou.

This tea is made in Qiangang, a small village on Mt. Fuzhi in Zhejiang province, not far from Pingshui, home of the more famous Gunpowder tea. The leaves are frosted with white hair on the back, and the buds are covered with hair so fine as to be hardly visible. The processed leaves are curled in a shape somewhere between the pellets of Gunpowder and the arc of Mei (Eyebrow) tea. In a cup the leaf-bud sets float point-upward like flagged spears. The sweet, fresh flavor of this tea is unforgettable.

It may be the particular method of processing that gives this tea its outstanding flavor. It is de-enzymized in a flat pan over strong heat. The pan is kept covered a great deal of the time, a process called smothering, so the heat reaches the leaves more through its upward passage than through contact with the pan. Thus the stalks and larger leaves change color, but the younger, greener leaves—and the flavor—are not affected. This process takes place twice in this sequence: panfiring, rolling, heat-drying, second rolling, second heat drying, second de-enzymizing by heat-drying in a glowing pan, and curing in a wooden chest after cooling and sorting. This process, known as the Qiangang de-enzymizing method had been adopted in many nearby locales.

Taiping Houkui, a Floating World

Known as the best of Anhui province's pointed green teas, Taiping Houkui is a delight both to drink and to look at. It has the flavor of orchids, although it is not strictly a scented tea. Or, rather, the leaves as they open are naturally scented by the myriad of wild cymbidium orchids that blossom all over the mountains just at that time. During infusion, the dark green leaves unfurl like colorful floating flowers, with a reddish center vein and pink side veins. To ensure that the leaves create this beautiful picture, sorting standards are extemely high, and all

abnormal, incomplete, or discolored leaf sets are picked out by hand.

Its name, Taiping Houkui (Houkeng Leader), comes from a place in Taiping county. Since its gold medal in the first rank at the 1915 Panama Pacific Exposition it has become world famous.

The leaves are processed through de-enzymizing by heat-drying, which takes a great deal of expertise. The processed leaves are straight, taut, and heavy, and pointed at both ends. They are noted for their ability to stand up through several infusions.

Taiping Houkui grows on the northern slopes of one range of the Huangshan Mountains, whose peaks crowd together like trees of a forest. Rain half the year and mist and clouds the rest, along with the shade of the northern slopes, provide ideal conditions for tender tea leaves.

As for the orchids, the higher the slope, the better they grow. Experiments have even shown that the presence of the orchid flavor in the teas from orchid regions is in direct ratio to the altitude of the plantations.

Tianmu Qingding (Tianmu Green Summit), From the Very Top

The two main peaks of Mt. Tianmu (Eyes Looking Heavenward), East and West Tianmu, are each topped by a pool that never dries up, hence the name. They are located directly west of Hangzhou near the western edge of Zhejiang province. The mountain is famous for its natural resources and scenery of waterfalls and streams. The warm, moist climate that enables it to be the home of numerous rare animals and birds and many kinds of plants also makes the area a good tea producer. Its tea occupies a very important place in China's tea production. With bamboo shoots and walnuts, tea is prized as one of the "three treasures of Tianmu."

The tea bushes grow in the valleys, where it is misty three-fourths of the year. Tianmu Qingding tea is mainly from the cloud and mist belt, between 1600 and 4000 feet. The summit is too windy to grow tea. The processed leaves are tight, dark green strips with visible hair and many leaf-bud sets.

Qingding tea is also used for scenting as Jasmine and Yulan (Magnolia) tea.

Tunlu (Tunxi Green), a Time-Honored Name

The name Tunlu is a contraction for Tunxi Green, referring to various teas well known on the Hongkong and foreign markets since early in this century. Tunxi is a mountain city located where the southernmost corner of Anhui province meets Zhejiang and Jiangxi provinces. Once, all the tea from a large surrounding area in the three provinces was brought there for processing and shipping. Since 1949 some of the areas have been producing tea under their own names, including Wulu and Suilu (Wuyuan county, Jiangxi and Sui'an, once a county in Zhejiang).

Tunlu tea may still be remembered in some countries by the names under which it was once known: Special Tribute in Russia, Chunmee (Chunmei, Zhenmei, Precious Eyebrow) and Oolong Chunmee in Europe, and Fengmei (Phoenix Eyebrow), E'mei (Moth's Eyebrow), and Xiamu (Shrimp's Eyes) in the U.S.

In 1960 the varieties were renamed in order of quality as: Chunmee, fine taut, eyebrow-shaped strips with strong fragrance and mellow taste, outstanding among green teas and popular both in China and abroad; Gongxi (Tribute to Emperor Kang Xi), shaped like grains of various sizes; Xiumei (Elegant Eyebrow); and Fuxi (Supplementary Tribute).

Weishan Maojian (Hairpoint), Smoked for Xinjiang

We include this tea because of its uniqueness, even though it is not generally available abroad. The bright yellow leaves are a highly valued gift in Xinjiang, where it is drunk after a meal of mutton to help digest the fat.

It is grown on Mt. Weishan in Ningxiang county, south of Dongting Lake in north central Hunan province. Two processes differ from the usual: the leaves are withered in an airtight container so that they turn a glossy yellow color, and then later they are cured in smoke from the *xianhuang* vine or maple wood. The beverage is clear, yellow-orange with a smoky flavor.

White Tea (Baihao Yinzhen, White Down Silver Needles)

It sounds rather fabulous, and indeed it is, for this tea consists of nothing but buds, which are covered with whitish hairs. A rare tea produced only in China, chiefly in Fujian province, it originally came from wild mountain trees. The connoisseurs seem to have been seeking the ultimate, and tender young leaves were not fine enough for them, so they sought to get the leaves while they were still more delicate, before they had even burst from the bud.

The Song dynasty "Tea Emperor" Hui Zong wrote that white tea has the rarest and most delicate flavor. He called it a special kind different from all others, but some people now consider it a form of green tea.

White tea has now become more widely available, often sold as Silvery Tip Pekoe, a form of its traditional name, and now also under the simpler designations China White and Fujian White. Its main area of production is Jianyang county in northern Fujian province.

When the buds are fully grown in spring, just before they open, they are plucked from the ends of the branches, along with a few attached leaves. Buds an inch long are picked out for first quality tea. The leaves are from two strains, Shui Hsien (Water Sprite) and Dai Bai (Dabai, Big White).

Rolling and fermenting are not part of this tea's processing. The leaves are de-enzymized by steaming. When they are infused, the buds stand upright like a forest of stalagmites in the cup. The pale yellow brew has a mellow, sweet taste.

The smaller buds and leaves become raw material for the Pai Mu Tan (Baimudan, White Peony) and Show Mee (Shoumei, Longevity Eyebrow) varieties. The bulk White Peony looks like a lot of tiny bouquets, with clusters of small round white flowers surrounded by gray-green leaves. They produce a clear orange-yellow beverage. This is also a rare tea. The Show Mee silvery leaves produce a light brownish orange drink with a sweet taste.

White tea is held to be particularly valuable for lowering heat, combating the influence of dampness, and stimulating the intestinal tract.

Xinyang Maojian, Hairpoint from Henan's Xinyang

Henan's Xinyang prefecture has been famous for its Maojian tea since the Tang dynasty. Today it is one of the country's most thriving areas of agricultural and sideline production, quite often visited and written about, so its tea is being sampled by more people.

Though Xinyang is on the edge of the arid North China plain, the mountainous southern and western parts, crisscrossed by streams and brooks, have plenty of the clouds and mist needed for good tea. The processed leaves are in fine, taut strips. They yield a beverage with a chestnut flavor and a long-lasting aftertaste. This tea has been produced with only very simple equipment. What makes it different are the skillful hand movements of rolling, adjusted to the heat and softness or dryness of the tender leaves.

Not much is exported, but the tea can be bought locally and in Zhengzhou and Kaifeng in the province, and in large cities like Beijing, Wuhan, and Tianjin.

Xishan, a Bright Green Tea

This clear dark-green tea is named for Mt. Xishan in the southwestern part of the Guangxi Zhuang autonomous region, noted for its fantastic mountains that poke abruptly out of the plain. Xishan (Western Mountain) tea, one of Guangxi's several varieties, is a longtime export product, and won a second prize at the 1915 Panama Pacific Exposition.

Here the season lasts from February to November, and each year can sustain twenty to thirty pluckings of the small, hairy leaves of the low tea bushes. A special process of roasting and rolling them three times produces a fine, taut leaf which yields a bright green drink of exceptional fragrance.

Other Guangxi varieties include Liupao (Liubao, see p. 153), Guiping (county) Xishan, and Nanshan and Lingyun Baimao (White Down, see p. 133). In its highest misty uplands this region also produces a Yunwu (Cloud and Mist) tea.

Yinzhen, Yinfeng (Silver Needles, Silverpoint)

The pale yellow shafts of Yinzhen (Silver Needles) were tribute tea from Tang on through Qing times. Their very special processing takes three days. Only fat, tender, white-haired buds are used. They are roasted at 90 degrees Fahrenheit (32 degrees centigrade) until 70 percent dry, then wrapped in brown paper and stored for two days in wooden cases. Then they undergo a second roasting at low heat, and are again wrapped to be stored for one day. After a final heating the tea is packed in metal chests, where it keeps exceptionally well.

The yellow-orange beverage is extremely fragrant. The upward-pointing buds floating upright in it have been likened to emerging bamboo shoots.

Yinzhen is produced on Mt. Junshan, situated in Yueyang county on a beautiful peninsula in Dongting Lake in the south-central province of Hunan. In the late 1950s, tea technicians in Changsha county around the provincial capital created a new tea combining the Yinzhen method with others. They called it Yinfeng (Silverpoint).

With this new process, the buds are kneaded and rubbed into fine strips in large woks at low heat until the white hairs are clearly visible. This step is called "raising the white hair." Then they are cooled and again heated until fully dry. This requires less time than the process for Silver Needles, but the clear, fragrant light green tea is highly appreciated.

Yongxi Huoqing (Yongxi Fire Green)

This Ming dynasty tribute tea comes in tiny, slightly hairy, dark green pellets somewhat like those of Gunpowder tea. It has an unusual orchid fragrance absorbed from nearby cymbidium orchids blooming as its leaves open. Jingxian county of Xuancheng prefecture south of the Yangtze in eastern Anhui province is its home.

Yuhua Tea and the Legend of Rainflower Terrace

Clear green, mellow-tasting Yuhua (Rainflower) gets its name from a legend. In ancient times Master Yun Guang, an eminent monk, usually taught the Buddhist scriptures on a certain hill in the city of Nanjing, in Jiangsu province northwest of Shanghai. He taught so well that God was pleased and sent a shower of flowers down after every good sermon. The flowers turned into the many multicolored pebbles that can be found on the hill. People collect and display them in a bowl of water, which enhances their color. The place became known as Rainflower Terrace.

Jiangsu province has produced famous teas since Tang times. When its tea company decided to launch a new product in 1958, Yuhua was the logical name. The leaves are straight like pine needles and the clear green beverage has a mellow taste.

Yulu, Green Jade or Jade Dew for Japan

This famous tea is indeed a deep, glossy green color as its name, Jade Green, implies. In ages past, the Japanese learned the process for Green Jade, which remains one of their important teas. The Chinese variety is sometimes known as Wufeng Yulu for its place of origin, Mt. Wufeng (Five-Peak Mountain) in southwestern Hubei province.

What is different about this tea is that the leaves are not withered, but are first de-enzymized by a minute of steaming over hot water. This enables them to keep their fresh color. The picked leaves must be processed as soon as possible, preferably the same day. After steaming they are air-dried and cooled, panfried to remove remaining water and rawness, then rolled at low heat until fully dry. The fine, taut rolls of the finished tea look like pine needles. The fragrant beverage is a clear green.

This tea is sold to Japan, the United States, and Hongkong. A similar product is exported to Japan by Zhejiang province under the name Steamed Green.

Hubei has been a famous producer of tea since the Tang dynasty. In the seventeenth and eighteenth centuries, the Yangtze River city of Hankou, one of the three that make up the metropolis of Wuhan, became a leading tea shipping port. Another famous tea that passes through it is Yihong Black (Yi is an old name for Hunan province, which lies south of Hubei). Yihong is produced around Eshi in eastern Hunan and is exported to Southeast Asia, North Africa, and Britain. Hubei Black is sold in Egypt, Pakistan, and the United States.

Zisun (Purple Bamboo Shoot)

A vintage tribute in the Tang dynasty, today this green tea brings a high price on some foreign markets and is also very popular in China. It is named for the appearance of its plump, pointed buds which remind people of bamboo. At plucking time the stalks are pink and the buds white. Zisun is grown on Mt. Guzhu near the southern shore of Lake Taihu in the northernmost part of Zhejiang province. So this clear, yellow-green tea with a sweet aftertaste is also known as Guzhu Zisun or Huzhou Zisun.

BLACK TEAS (HONG CHA, RED TEA)

In addition to the special brands below, many black teas are sold on the foreign market simply by the name of the province. These include Fujian Black (Minhong), Guangdong Black, Guizhou Black, Hainan Black, Hunan Black (Yihong), Sichuan Black (Chuanhong), and Yunnan Black (Dianhong).

Hainan Black

Now widely sold abroad, this product is one of China's great black teas. The processed leaves have tan tips highlighted amid the black of the loose leaves. It makes a strong drink with a heavy fragrance. Hainan, the great subtropical island off China's southern coast, has ideal conditions for growing tea, with high mountains and abundant rainfall. Many large tea plantations have been laid out in Hainan in recent decades.

Jiuqu Hongmei (Nine-Bend Red Plum) or Jiuqu Wulong (Black Dragon)

Jiuqu Hongmei tea ranks with the famous Keemun Black in quality. Its leaves twist into fine, tight, hook-like rolls, and produce a beverage as bright as their Red Plum name.

The name Jiuqu means Nine-Bend Stream, a main area of this tea's production near Mt. Dawu in Zhejiang province. The mountain faces the wide Qiantang River, famous for its tidal bore, so plenty of ocean moisture is drawn up to the tea gardens. Hongmei from the Nine-Bend area is ranked as first grade, with that from other parts of Zhejiang second and third.

When thunder rolls over Nine-Bend Stream, the people tell this story to their children: A couple living by a stream had a child late in life. They treasured the fine, strong boy above all else. One day while playing at the brook he found a beautiful black pearl. He put it in his mouth to keep it safe and ran home to show his parents, but on the way he tripped over a stone and swallowed the pearl.

Soon he was rolling on the ground with severe stomach pain. Suddenly a violent thunderstorm came up. The boy changed into a black dragon and flew up into the sky, where he remained a long time riding the clouds and rain, reluctant to leave his parents. From time to time he would turn and look back at them. He made altogether nine turns. When he was gone, there remained a stream with nine bends.

That is why this tea is sometimes called Jiuqu Wulong (Black Dragon). It is a fully-fermented *gongfu* black tea, but because of this name it is sometimes confused with the semi-fermented oolong (wulong).

Keemun (Qihong), the Champagne of Black Teas

The name Keemun comes from Qimen county in southern Anhui province, where almost all the mountains are covered with tea bushes. It is a variety of black tea, and since all black tea is known as red tea in Chinese, the Chinese name is Qihong. For taste Keemun is considered matchless, a flavor that almost sings. Its fragrance, known throughout the tea trade as the "Keemun aroma," has been compared to that of the orchid or rose.

Qimen county produced only green tea until the 1880s. It owes the change to a young civil official who lost his position when his superior fell into disgrace. Then he remembered his father's advice, which he had disregarded in his pride at passing the exam and becoming an official: a skill is a better guarantor of a living than precarious officialdom.

The young man went to Fujian and learned the black tea process. On his return he set up three factories using the new technique on the same leaves his neighbors were making into green tea. The method was perfectly suited to the leaves, produced by the loose, easily drained soil and the area's warm, moist climate. His first product in 1875, fine, dark-green strips with a distinctive flavor, hit a wave of black tea popularity in England. Soon other local factories switched to black.

Keemun became world renowned and captured the black tea market from India's Darjeeling. In 1915 Keemun was another Chinese winner at the Panama Pacific International Exposition. Though in recent years tea connoisseurs have taken more to broken black, Keemun black has held its own and remains the "king of red (black) teas."

Keemun is originally one of the congou-type teas. That is, it requires a great deal of *gongfu* (disciplined skill) to make into fine, taut strips without breaking the leaves.

Lapsang Souchong (Zengshan Xiaozhong),the Smoked Tea

The souchongs, smoked teas with a distinctive flavor sometimes described as tarry, are a special product of Fujian province. The Fukienese word *souchong (xiao zhong)* means "subvariety," that is, a subvariety of the black teas from the Wuyi Mountains in Fujian. This tea is also sold as Fujian Black Lapsang Souchong.

Legend claims that the smoking process was discovered by accident. During the Qing dynasty, an army unit passing through Xingcun (Star Village) camped in a tea factory filled with fresh leaves awaiting processing. When the soldiers left and the workers could get back into the premises, they realized that to arrive at market in time, it was too late to dry the leaves the usual way. So they lit open fires of pine wood to hasten the drying. Not only did the tea reach the market in time, but the smoked pine flavor created a sensation. A new product was born.

The leaves are first withered over fires of pine or cypress wood. After panfrying and rolling, they are pressed into wooden barrels and covered with cloth to ferment until they give off a pleasant fragrance. The leaves are fried again and rolled into taut strips. Then they are placed in bamboo baskets and hung on wooden racks over smoking pine fires to dry and absorb the smoke flavor. When finished they are thick, glossy black strips, and produce a bright red beverage with a unique aroma. It is drunk with or without sugar and milk.

This tea is sometimes sold as Zhengshan Souchong. As sales abroad expanded, the demand for Wuyi teas exceeded the supply and many fake Wuyi teas were marketed. Therefore, the authentic Wuyi vendors began calling theirs Zhengshan Souchong (Real Wuyi Subvariety). The name seems to have traveled a long way to become Lapsang Souchong—a favorite of Sherlock Holmes and several other fictional Britons.

Pouchong, (Pao Zhong, Baozhong), Popular in Taiwan

The name means "the wrapped kind." Several varieties of teas are wrapped in paper while they cure after drying. Pouchong tea originated in Fujian and was taken to Taiwan, where a variety named Wenshan Pouchong is quite popular. The tea is wrapped in five-ounce packs in paper made from cotton, and dried by baking.

Although Pouchong is sold as green tea, it is lightly fermented, therefore technically no longer green tea. Fermentation time is shorter than for oolong. Thus Pouchong is actually a fourth category, ranking between green and oolong on the fermentation scale. It is made chiefly in Taiwan from the long, thin Fujian-type leaf. It is sometimes used as a base for Jasmine tea.

Yingteh (Yingde) Black

In 1956 the Chinese government decided to build a tea plantation on a stretch of wasteland outside the county town of Yingde in northern Guangdong province. It was planted with tea shrubs of the Yunnan big-leaf and Fenghuang Shuixian varieties. A modern processing plant and tea research institute were set up. Their product became known as Yingteh tea.

Since its initial export in 1959, this product has joined the ranks of the world's finest black teas, and is said to be comparable to those of India and Sri Lanka.

This tea is a glossy black, with visible golden hair. The leaves are rolled into granules which yield a mellow-tasting, brownish-red liquor. Yingteh is sold as Broken Black tea in tea bags.

Yunnan Black (Dianhong), from Ancient Roots

Tea has been produced in Yunnan for 1700 years, according to ancient records of her Dai nationality, people of the same ethnic stock as the Thais in nearby Thailand. Yunnan Black derives its name Dianhong

(Dian Black) from Dian, another name for the Yunnan area. As noted earlier, in Chinese "black" tea is called *hong* (red) tea.

The tea plant itself is often considered a native of Yunnan, for 260 of its total 320 varieties are found there, including some extraordinary ancient tea trees (see p. 77). Tea is grown all over Xishuangbanna, an autonomous prefecture in Yunnan's far south, home of the Dai and many others of China's minority nationalities. Well known for centuries have been the Six Tea Mountains in Xishuangbanna and the Simao prefecture to its north.

The Yunnan blacks are produced from a strain of ancient native Yunnan Dayeh (broad-leafed) tea tree used for the famous medicinal Pu-erh tea (see p. 154). Such trees grow along the Lancang River in the Xishuangbanna autonomous prefecture in the far south of Yunnan province. They have a longer lifespan, earlier and stronger buds, fat shoots, and thick, soft leaves.

Yunnan Black, or Yunnan Congou, processed from these leaves since 1939, has become one of the fine teas on the international market. It has long been sold in quantity to the Soviet Union and Eastern Europe and is now also marketed in Western Europe, North America, and other areas. The bulk tea consists of the leaves accompanied by a profusion of fat golden buds.

Also exported to these areas is Yunnan Broken Black, produced since 1960 and said to be on a par with the finest of the Indian Assam teas. It is characterized by its aromatic flavor and brisk (some use the word "spicy") flavor. The most famous kind is Flowery Broken Orange Pekoe (F.B.O.P.). Broken Black can be distinguished from Congou by its broken leaves, as distinguished from strips.

OOLONG TEAS

Oolong tea is believed to have originated in the Wuyi Mountains along the western border of Fujian province, and has been exported from there since the eighteenth century. These mountains are noted for their ninety-nine grotesque cliffs and thirty-six peaks, all of which are said to be covered with green tea bushes.

Though oolong tea is now also manufactured elsewhere, this area is still one of the biggest producers. Wu-yi Yen (Wuyi Yan, Wuyi Cliffs) tea is a large general category for several kinds of oolong. They are easy to recognize from the appearance of the leaves during infusion. The stout, crinkled leaves, when immersed in water, become bright green in the center and slowly turn red around the edges, the result of their partial fermentation. The most famous kinds are Wuyi Shui Hsien, Mingcong Qizhong (Famous Rare Orchid), Dahongpao, and Rougui. Wu-yi Yen teas are also sold under such names as Wuyi Chen Chung (Zhenzhong), Wuyi Liu Hsiang (Liuxiang), Wuyi Min Chung (Mingzhong), and Wuyi Chi Chung (Qizhong).

Dahongpao (Scarlet Robe)

Three big Chinese characters *Da Hong Pao* (Big Red Robe) proclaim themselves boldly from a rock on a steep and rugged crag near Tianxin Cliff in the Wuyi Mountains of Fujian province. On a patch of flat land before the rock grow a few clumps of three-foot-high tea bushes with leaves a bit thicker than usual and slightly pinkish buds.

Here the sun shines only in the morning. In the afternoon the shadow of the rock keeps the hot sun off the bushes, so the buds remain tender. The water from a small, slow stream of a nearby spring seeps through the sandy soil to make this an ideal place for growing fine tea. Legend says this is the location of the bushes whose leaves became famous for their healing properties.

At some distant time, possibly the Ming dynasty, for this tea has been known since then, the magistrate of Chong'an county had a chronic illness, unidentified in the story about him. But after a period of drinking tea from these bushes, reputed for their medicinal qualities, he recovered. So grateful was he that he came to burn incense at the spot. Then as a token of respect, he hung his red magisterial robe on one of the bushes—and ever after that the tea bore this name.

There are other versions of the name's origin. One is that a Ming dynasty official supervising picking in the area took off his robe and hung it up when he climbed a tree. If so, he must have been an unusual official. The second, equally unlikely, is that the monks of Tianxin Temple, who maintained the (then taller) tea trees, trained monkeys to pick the high leaves, and because they were doing it for the emperor, dressed them in red.

Whatever the origin of the name, the belief in Dahongpao as an aid to health and longevity remained constant. In old China, high officials and wealthy people would rush for the tea as soon as it came in season, and bid the price up, because it was in short supply and quickly sold out. Now more is produced, from other bushes of the same type.

Fonghwang Tan-chung (Fenghuang Dancong or Select)

The single trunk rises straight up, and the branches open out like an umbrella. Pickers must use tall ladders or climb up into the leafy tops. These trees, which yield the leaves for Fonghwang Tan-chung oolong tea, are specimens of the Fenghuang Shuixian strain which have been selected for careful breeding as straight-trunk trees. The name Fonghwang Tan-chung means Fenghuang Select. Fenghuang (Phoenix) is the name of a mountain near the coast in northeastern Guangdong province. This tea is believed to have been a tribute tea in the Song dynasty.

During infusion, the long golden-brown strips of processed leaves sharply reveal their oolong characteristics by turning a pronounced green in the center and brownish red around the edges. The clear, orange-brown beverage has a strong natural aroma. The first taste is somewhat bitter, but this tea is valued for its durable infusion and long-lasting pleasant aftertaste.

The people of the nearby Shantou (Swatow) area are known for their particular way with these leaves for *gongfu* tea (tea brewed with great skill). They make it strong, using miniature tea sets with a small teapot and tiny cups the size of a half-walnut. Particular attention is paid to cleanliness and quality of water. The first infusion is one minute. The second one of three minutes is the best time for savoring the mellow taste, sip by sip. The third may take five minutes, but many think that this infusion is too weak.

Liubao, the Energizer

Popular in damp tropical regions, Liubao tea is often cited by the overseas Chinese of Southeast Asia as the reason that Chinese, with it as a stimulant, can work energetically in such climates while others feel enervated. It is also used to aid digestion, eliminate fats, and combat the effects of dampness. The name comes from its place of origin, the town of Liubao in Cangwu county in the Guangxi Zhuang autonomous region. Some is also grown in western Guangdong province.

This tea falls between the oolong and black categories, for it is fermented longer than oolong but less than black. The leaves, stacked to ferment overnight, turn a glossy black. After fermentation, heat-drying and sorting, they are softened by steaming. Then they are packed in wicker baskets, pressed in tightly around the edges and more loosely in the center to facilitate air-drying, which takes two months.

The leaves can be stored for a long time. In fact they are considered at their best when they are covered with a light golden mold. The deep reddish-brown brew has a full-bodied flavor that has been likened to that of betelnuts. This tea is quite popular in Hongkong and Macao.

Pu-erh (P'u-erh, Pu'er), a Famous Medicinal Tea

This tea is famed for its medicinal properties. The leaves come from the Yunnan province Dayeh (large-leaf) variety of broad-leafed tea tree, which may be more closely related to the original ancient tea tree of pre-glaciation times than the smaller-leaved one. It is marketed in bulk as Pu-erh, shaped into cakes as Pu'er Cake Tea and into the bowl-shaped cakes called Yunnan Tuo Cha. (Tuo Cha can also be green.)

The peoples of the Yunnan-Tibet border have drunk Pu-erh since the Tang dynasty, according to a Song dynasty scientific reference. The troops of Kublai Khan, "pacifying" the southwest after the thirteenth century Mongol conquest, are said to have introduced Pu-erh to the rest of China for its medicinal value.

Tea from these high mountains has traditionally been carried in shoulder baskets through primeval forests (now there are hairpin-curve roads) for processing and sale in the tea market at the county town of Pu'er. Located in central south Yunnan, Pu'er county itself does not grow tea, but the name it has given to this variety has become internationally known.

Pu-erh is often taken for relief of indigestion and diarrhea. Modern medical tests indicate its effectiveness in reducing cholesterol (see p. 105). Pu-erh is customarily kept for a long time, and in Asian tradition leaves with a light coating of mold are considered the best and to have the greatest medicinal effect. However, tests in two universities and a medical center in Japan showed no significant difference between two- and twenty-year-old Pu-erh in reducing cholesterol.

Pu-erh is viewed as a mild tea, suitable for young and old, and for persons with strong or weak constitutions. Yunnan Tuo Cha, a form of Pu-erh, received the Ninth International Food Award at a conference in Barcelona, Spain, in 1986.

Pu-erh is very special because of a unique combination of factors. It is an unusual large-leafed variety, it enjoys special growing conditions with the combination of climate and soil in the Yunnan mountains, and it is semi-fermented, but for a longer time than oolong.

The taste has been described as mellow, however those not accustomed to it might not enjoy the "old"—perhaps "elemental" or "earthy" are better words—taste, particularly in the first infusion. For others, however, this flavor will add to its aura of wonder, and seem fitting in a tea prized for its medicinal properties. Some people recommend first getting used to Nuoshan Pu'er, which has less of this taste. Or Pu-erh may be mixed with a little Yinzhen (see p. 144) to cut the "old" flavor and create an unexpected new one. Pu-erh is known for maintaining flavor through multiple infusions.

A combination of Pu-erh and Chrysanthemum tea (made from the small pale yellow blossoms of that plant) is considered particularly good for cooling internal heat, and is also delicious. Called Gupu cha, it can be requested in Cantonese teahouses as Gook Po cha.

Another famous Cantonese specialty is Pu-Show (Pu-erh and Show Mee). The latter, a white tea, is classified as "cool" by traditional pharmacology, and is sometimes neutralized with a combination that also yields a new flavor.

Pu-erh tea is sold loose (of these, Nuoshan from the mountain of the same name is the best known), or in pressed form named for the shape in which a block is molded. These include:

Tuocha, bowl tea, shaped by pressing into a bowl.

Bingcha (Beeng Cha), cake tea. It comes in large and small stacks of seven layers, thus sometimes called Qi Zi (Seven Sons), and sold in Hongkong, Macao and Southeast Asia. Small-size cakes are consumed by the Tibetan people.

Tuancha, ball tea, in ping-pong ball size and up. Balls of this tea used for tribute were the size of a head, and it was called Head Tea.

Fangcha (square), and *Pu-erh Zuncha* (rectangular).

Yunnan has three plucking seasons, which provide the names for special kinds of Pu-erh:

Chunjian (Spring Pointed) plucked between Qingming and the Grain Rain (roughly April 5 to 15). It has abundant fine, long white hair.

Ershui (Second Crop) plucked from early June to July. These fat, juicy leaves are made into pressed tea.

Guhua (Grain Flower) plucked between Bailu (White Dew) and Shuang Jiang (Frost Descends) in October. With plenty of fine, white hair, it is used to make cake tea.

Shui Hsien (Shuixian, Water Sprite)

Known for its natural orchidlike flavor and long-lasting aftertaste, this tea and Ti Kwan Yin are the two leading types of oolong semi-fermented tea. It is named for the special strain of the tea plant from which it is made. The discovery of the latter was a lucky accident for both those who enjoy this tea and for tea culture as a whole.

Over a thousand years ago a type of tall, large-leafed tea tree was noted at Dahu prefecture in west-central Fujian province. Its domestication, however, began only three hundred years ago.

Around the turn of the eighteenth century a large tea tree was found growing lying on the ground, pressed under the fallen wall of a run-down temple. From beneath it several small shoots had developed and taken root. A tea grower from southern Fujian who had migrated to the Dahu area took an interest in them and transplanted some to his garden. They produced a fine tea, and also taught him that tea plants could be reproduced by layering. Both the strain and the method quickly spread to the nearby Wuyi Mountains and other areas.

The meaning of the word *shuixian* is "water sprite," also the Chinese name for the narcissus. The coastal city of Quanzhou (Chuanzhou), through which this tea was traditionally exported, is famous for its narcissi, themselves an important export product.

The Shuixian strain has a single trunk and sparse branches. Its thick leaves are a glossy dark green, and it has lots of fat, greenish-yellow buds covered with hair. The leaves, processed into loose, twisted strips, are good for many infusions of the clear, bright orange-brown beverage. The leaves can also be processed into black tea and white tea. It is popular in southeastern China as an early-morning drink or served with dim sum brunch.

Wuyi Shui Hsien (also called Wuyi Hsiencha) is the most famous of the Shui Hsien type. Another variety from Yongchun, Anxi and their neighboring areas is loosely grouped as Min Nan Shui Xian (Southern Fujian Shui Hsien). This tea is also grown in Taiwan and in Guangdong. The products of the latter, under the names Fonghwang Tan-chung and Fenghuang Shui Hsien, are popular in Hongkong and Macao as well as Guangdong.

Ti Kwan Yin (Tieguanyin), Tea of the Iron Bodhisattva

This is the most famous of all Chinese oolongs. Guanyin, sometimes called the Goddess of Mercy, is actually more like the Buddhist equivalent of the Madonna. She is a bodhisattva, one who is qualified to enter nirvana, but chose to remain on earth to bring all to enlightenment. Statues of her stand in many Buddhist temples, and a woman who wants a child may pray to her. A legend gives one version of why a tea bears her name.

An iron statue of Guanyin stood in a rundown temple in central Fujian's Shaxian (Sand county). The temple's condition aroused the concern of a tea grower who passed it daily. Financially unable to repair it, he thought that the least he could do was to burn incense and clean the place twice a month.

One night Guanyin appeared to him in a dream and told him to look in the cave behind the temple for a treasure. He was to take it for himself but also to share it with others. There he found a single tea shoot which he planted and cultivated into a bush with leaves that produced a singularly fine drink. He began selling it under the Guanyin name, and gave many cuttings to his neighbors. All prospered, and eventually the temple was repaired.

A book from contemporary China gives another version: this tea is so named for the appearance of its processed leaves—dark as iron and heavier than other teas, but with a quality as pure and beautiful as Guanyin.

Tieguanyin is also the name of a tea strain. The short, spreading shrub has glossy, dark green leaves, soft and fat with curling serrated edges. The tightly twisted, shiny dark green leaves produce an aromatic brownish-orange liquor of high astringency. These leaves can be used through many more infusions than most varieties.

This is the tea that the people of Chaozhou on the Guangdong province coast like to brew *gongfu* style in tiny pottery teapots and sip from thimble-sized cups, the better to savor its orchidlike flavor and long-lasting aftertaste.

A related oolong also made in Fujian and exported is Ti Lohan (Tielohan, Iron Arhat, a monk who has put aside all the passions of the world). It comes from from Hui'an, and is particularly famous in the Philippines.

SCENTED TEAS

Green teas lend themselves well to scenting, and are used for the most famous scented brands. A few black teas are also scented. When flower scent is used with black tea, the blossoms are usually pounded to a powder, which is mixed with the tea leaves. Scented teas often have the word *hua* (flower) in the name.

Three of the main ways of naming scented teas are:

1. By flowers used in scenting: The designation *huacha* (flower tea) is added to the names of teas, for instance Chulan Huacha (Zhulan or *Chloranthus spicatus*). It is also added to Daidai (*Citrus aurantium*, Canton orange), Guihua (*Osmanthus fragrans*, similar to cinnamon), Moli (Jasmine), Youzi (Pomelo Blossom), Yulan (Magnolia), and Zhizi (Cape Jasmine). There is also Meigui Hongcha (Rose Congou or Rose-scented Black).

2. By names of crude tea used in scenting: The word *hua* is prefixed to various kinds of tea. Examples: Huapilochun, Huadafang, Huahongqing, Hualongjing, Huamaofeng, and Hua Oolong.

3. By the name of fruit used in scenting, of which Lichee Black (Lizhi Hongcha) is the best known.

Below are more detailed descriptions of a few scented teas.

Jasmine (Moli Huacha)

Tea enriched with the fragrance of jasmine flowers has been a favorite since the Southern Song dynasty. Jasmine (*Jasminium sambac*), a native of the Persian Gulf area, was brought to southern China sometime before the third century A.D., according to a Chinese botanist of that time.

Because the sweet-smelling jasmine blooms open only at night, that is when processing must go on. The flowers, plucked in the morning when they are freshest, are kept in a cool place until nightfall. Then, just as they are about to open and release their fragrance, they are piled in a given ratio next to previously heaped piles of heat-dried green tea leaves. The loose, dry leaves absorb the fragrance.

After several hours, when the piles of tea start to heat up, the leaves are spread out and re-piled for another round of scenting. Ordinary grades of tea are scented two or three times, special grades up to seven times.

The kilogram ratio of jasmine to tea is 50:42.5 for first grade tea. For special grades, the same amount of tea takes 75 to 100 kilograms of blossoms. Then the tea leaves are refired to remove the moisture of the blossoms so that they do not mold.

In some places this scenting is done in wooden chests, with layers of flowers alternating with those of leaves. Much of the labor of piling the leaves has now been taken over by mixing machines and electric driers, so that tea of more uniform quality and a more accessible price can be produced.

Sometimes jasmine flowers can be found in the tea when it is sold, but this is not an indicator of higher quality. In fact, it may mean a lower quality because the flowers are carefully removed from the better teas. The quality of Jasmine tea is determined by the quality of green tea and the effectiveness of scenting.

The jasmine flavor of the beverage is so pronounced that Chinese custom deems it a good tea to serve with strong-tasting foods. Some recommend it for counteracting fish and mutton odors. Oolong tea can also be scented with jasmine, and the result is a tea with a strong aftertaste.

Li Shizhen wrote in his 1578 pharmacopoeia that jasmine has both soothing and warming properties. Jasmine tea, presumably containing some buds, is held to relieve diarrhea. This tea is very popular in north China, but some southerners say it does not soothe the throat or quench thirst as well as regular green tea or oolong.

The Fuzhou area in Fujian province is the most famous producer of Jasmine tea. The jasmine shrub grows particularly well along the Min River, where fields of it fill the evening air with fragrance. Jasmine tea is also produced at Suzhou and Nanjing in Jiangsu province, Hangzhou and Jinhua in Zhejiang province, and in Sichuan, Jiangsi, Anhui, and Hubei provinces. One brand famous in China and abroad is Jinhua Moli Maofeng (Jinhua Jasmine Hairpoint) made in Zhejiang province by scenting leaves of fine Maofeng tea (see p. 132). Jasmine Oolong is created by scenting oolong tea.

Lanhsiang (Lanxiang), Orchid-Scented

Made of high-grade green tea scented with the flowers of the *Chloranthus spicatus*, this bright red brew with a rich fragrance is one of China's famous teas and a product of Guangdong province.

Lichee Black (Lizhihong), Fruit-Flavored

A black tea treated with the juice of the lichee produces a delightful beverage. The fresh, juicy lichee is one of south China's famous fruits. For smoothness and color its flesh is often likened to white jade. The sweet-tart taste, color, and juiciness of lichees remind some Westerners of grapefruit, although the two fruits are not related. In the present Chinese spelling they are *lizhi*. (Alternative spellings seen in the West include *litchee* and *lychee*.) Guangdong province is a big producer of lichees and Lichee Black tea.

The Chinese people often recall a bit of their history in connection with lichees. They were a favorite of Lady Yang Yuhuan, considered one of the four most beautiful women in Chinese history. She was the beloved of Tang dynasty Emperor Xuan Zong (also known as Ming Huang, r. 712–756). By paying too much attention to her (she is also known as Yang Guifei, Honored Concubine Yang) and not enough to state affairs, he lost his throne.

He would do anything to make her happy. Lichees are an extremely perishable fruit, so the emperor arranged to have them brought to his capital Xi'an from the south by night and day relay riders. To this day the fruit is also known by the name Feizi Xiao (Feizi's Smile).

Rose Congou (Meigui Hongcha, Rose-scented Black)

This popular product made with rose petals is exported from Guangdong and some other provinces.

IN SUMMARY

What's a good tea to serve with a specific food? Most teas can be served any time, but some have characteristics that make them particularly good in a certain role.

Jasmine	After strong tasting food, like seafood
Liuxi and Pu-erh	After a meal with a lot of fat
Black tea	With salty or sweet desserts
Biluochun	With salty desserts

And since this book emphasizes tea and your health, following is a summary of the main health benefits of these special teas, according to Chinese tradition. Many other teas, including black tea, can have similar effects (see chapter nine), but these below have been singled out by tradition.

Green Teas

Baihao Yinzhen (White Tea)	Stimulates digestive tract, counteracts dampness, heat
Gunpowder	Fluoride for teeth, bones
Liuxi, Pu-erh	Constipation, regularity, after heavy meal
Lu'an Guapian	Thirst quencher
Lung Ching	Hot weather cooler
Lushan Yunwu	Longevity
Mengding	Longevity, general good health
Puto Fo Cha	Diarrhea

Oolong and Scented

Dahongpao	Longevity, generally beneficial
Jasmine	Diarrhea
Liubao	Digestion, dampness, fats
Pu-erh	Digests fats, cuts cholesterol

A Seventeenth Century View of Tea: Garway's Broadsheet

Following is the text of the famous broadsheet or advertising leaflet circulated by coffeehouse proprietor Thomas Garway, the first to sell tea in England, with contemporary spelling, but today's punctuation.

The Drink is declared to be most wholesome, preserving in perfect health until extreme Old Age.

The particular virtues are these:

It maketh the Body active and lusty.

It helpeth the Head-ach, giddiness and heaviness thereof.

It removeth the Obstructions of the Spleen.

It is very good against the Stone and Gravel, cleansing the Kidneys and Uriters being drunk with Virgin's Honey instead of sugar.

It taketh away the difficulty of breathing, opening Obstructions.

It is good against Lipitude, Distillations, and cleareth the sight.

It removeth Lassitude, and cleareth and purifieth adult Humors and a hot Liver.

It is good against Crudities, strengthening the weakness of the Ventricle or Stomack, causing good Appetite and Digestion, and particularly for Men of corpulent Body and such as are the great eaters of Flesh.

It vanquisheth heavy Dreams, easeth the Brain, and strengtheneth the Memory.

It overcometh superfluous Sleep, and prevents Sleepiness in general, a draught of the Infusion being taken, so that without trouble whole nights may be spent in study without hurt to the Body, in that it moderately healeth and bindeth the mouth of the stomach.

163

It prevents and cures Agues, Surfets and Feavers, by infusing a fit quantity of the Leaf, thereby provoking a most gentle Vomit and breathing of the Pores, and hath been given with wonderful success.

It (being prepared with Milk and Water) strengtheneth the inward parts, and prevents consumption, and powerfully assuageth the pains of the Bowels, or griping of the Guts or Looseness.

It is good for Colds, Dropsies and Scurveys, if properly infused purging the Blood of Sweat and Urine, and expelleth Infection.

It driveth away all pains in the Collick proceeding from Wind, and purgeth safely the Gall.

And that the Virtues and Excellencies of this Leaf and Drink are many and great is evident and manifest by the high esteem and use of it (especially in later years) among the Physicians and knowing men of *France, Italy, Holland* and other parts of Christendom: and in England it had been sold in the Leaf for six pounds, and sometimes for ten pounds the pound weight, and in respect of its former scarceness and dearness, it hath been only used at *Regalia* in high Treatments and Entertainments, and Presents made thereof to Princes and Grandees till the year 1657. The said *Thomas Garway* did purchase a quantity thereof, and first publickly sold the said *Tea* in Leaf and Drink, made according to the directions of the most knowing Merchants and Travellers into Eastern Countries: And upon knowledge and experience of the said *Garway's* continued care and industry in obtaining the best *Tea*, and making Drink thereof, very many Noblemen, Physicians, Merchants and Gentlemen of Quality have ever since sent to him for the said Leaf and daily resort to his House in *Exchange Alley* aforesaid to drink the Drink thereof. And to the end that all Persons of Eminency and Quality, Gentlemen and others, who have occasion for *Tea* in Leaf may be supplied. These are given notice that the said *Thomas Garway* hath *Tea* to sell from sixteen to fifth Shillings the pound.

List of Teas Described

(Alphabetically by Market Name)

TEA NAME

Famous Teas by Provinces

This is a selective list. Not all teas described in this book appear here. When a kind is produced in several provinces, only the most famous are listed.

Anhui

Dafang, Huadafang, Huangshan Maofeng, Jinting Luxue, Keemun Black (Qihong), Lanhua, Lu'an Guapian, Taiping Houkui, Tunlu (Tunxi Green), Yongxi Huoqing

Fujian

NORTHERN FUJIAN (MIN BEI)

Chi Lan (Qilan, Rare Orchid), Dahongpao, Fujian Black (Minhong), Oolong, Jasmine (Moli Huacha), Mingcong Qizhong, Pai Mu Tan (Baimudan), Ro-guae (Rougui), Show Mee (Shoumei, Longevity), Shui Hsien (Shuixian), Taoren, Ti Kuan Yin (Tieguanyin), Ti Lohan (Tielohan), White tea (Baihao Yinzhen and Baimudan)

SOUTHERN FUJIAN (MIN NAM)

Chi Lan (Qilan, Rare Orchid), Jasmine (Moli Huacha), Lapsang Souchong (Zhengshan Xiaozhong), Mao Xie, Meishan Oolung, Show Mee (Shoumei), White tea (Baihao Yinzhen and Baimudan), Wuyi Black

Guangdong

Fonghwang Tan-chung (Fenghuang Dancong), Kooloo (Gulao), Lichee Black, Liupao (Liubao), Liuxi, Shui Hsien (Shuixian), Taoren, Ti Kwan Yin (Tieguanyin), Yingteh Black (Yinghong)

Guangxi Zhuang Autonomous Region

Baimao, Liupao (Liubao), Xishan

Guizhou

Duyun Maojian

Hainan

Hainan Black

Henan

Xinyang Maojian

Hubei

Black, Laoqing, Yihong Black, Yulu

Hunan

Anhua Songjian, Brick Tea, Hunan Black, Weishan Maojian, Xiangbolu, Yinfeng, Yinzhen, Yunfeng

Jiangsu

Jasmine (Moli Huacha), Pi Lo Chun (Biluochun), Yuhua

Jiangxi

Chunmee (Chunmei, Zhenmei), Lushan Yunwu, Ninghong (Nanjing and nearby areas), Wuyuan Mingmei

Shaanxi

Ziyang (Ziyang county)

Sichuan

E Ruizi (Emei Ruizi), Mengding, Sichuan Black (Chuanhong)

Taiwan

Tungting Oolong, Pouchong (Baozhong), Taiwan Black, Taiwan Oolung

Yunnan

Cake Tea (Southern Yunnan), Pressed Tea, Pu-erh (Puer), Tuocha, Yunnan Black (Dianhong), Yunnan Green (Dianlu)

Zhejiang

Huading Yunwu (Tiantai Yunwu), Huamaojian, Huangya, Huayuqian, Huiming, Jasmine (Moli Huacha), Jiande Baocha, Jinhua Moli Maofeng (Jinhua Jasmine Hairpoint), Jiukeng, Jiuqu Hongmei (Jiuqu Wulong), Lanxi Maofeng, Lung Ching (Longjing, Dragon's Well), Maojian, Mogan, Pingshui Gunpowder (Zhucha), Puto Fo Cha (Putuofo), Qiangang Huibai, Suilu, Tianmu Qingding, Tiantai Yunwu, Yandang Maofeng, Zisun

The Twenty-Four Solar Terms

Pinyin	Character	English	Gregorian Calendar Date
Lichun	立春	Spring Begins	February 5
Yushui	雨水	The Rains	February 19
Jingzhe	驚蟄	Insects Awaken	March 5
Chunfen	春分	Spring Equinox	March 20
Qingming	清明	Clear and Bright	April 5
Guyu	谷雨	Grain Rain	April 20
Lixia	立夏	Summer Begins	May 5
Xiaoman	小滿	Grain Fills Out	May 21
Mangzhong	芒種	Grain in Ear	June 6
Xiazhu	夏至	Summer Solstice	June 21
Xiaoshu	小暑	Small Heat	July 7
Dashu	大暑	Great Heat	July 23
Liqiu	立秋	Autumn Begins	August 7

Pinyin	Character	English	Gregorian Calendar Date
Chushu	處暑	Limit of Heat	August 23
Bailu	白露	White Dew	September 8
Qiufen	秋分	Autumn Equinox	September 23
Hanlu	寒露	Cold Dew	October 8
Shuangjiang	霜降	Frost Descends	October 23
Lidong	立冬	Winter Begins	November 7
Xiaoxue	小雪	Small Snow	November 22
Daxue	大雪	Great Snow	December 7
Dongzhi	冬至	Winter Solstice	December 21
Xiaohan	小寒	Small Cold	January 6
Dahan	大寒	Great Cold	January 26

Cantonese Names of Teas Described

(Alphabetically by Pinyin)

Known market names are listed. For other translations see text.

Pinyin	Character	Cantonese	Market Name
Baihao Yinzhen	白毛銀針	Bak Ho Ngan Jam	White
Baozhong	包種	Pauchong	Pouchong
Biluochun	碧螺春	Bik Lo Choon	Pi Lo Chun
Dafang	大紅袍	Dai Fong	
Dahongpao	大方	Dai Hung Po	
Dianhong	滇紅	Tin Hung	Yunnan Black
E Ruizi	娥蕊子	Ngor Yui Ji	Emei Ruizi
Fenghuang Dancong	鳳凰單叢	Fung Wong Taan Chung	Tanchong Fonghwang
Fengmei	鳳眉	Fung Mei	
Gulao	古勞	Koo Lou	Kooloo
Hainan Hong	海南紅茶		Hainan Black

Pinyin	Character	Cantonese	Market Name
Huading Yunwu	華頂雲霧	Wah Ding Wan Mo	
Huangshan Maofeng	黃山毛峯	Wong Shaan Mo Fung	
Huiming	惠明	Wai Ming	
Jingting Luxue	敬亭綠雪	Kin Ting Luk Suet	
Jiukeng	鳩坑	Kau Haang	
Jiuqu Hongmei	九曲紅梅	Kao Kuk	Hong Mei
Lanxi Maofeng	蘭溪毛峯	Laan Kai Mo Fung	
Lanxiang	蘭香		Lan-Hsiang
Lingyun Baimao	凌雲白毛	Ling Wan Back Hou	Lingyun White Down
Liubao	六堡	Luk Bo	Liupao
Liuxi	流溪	Lau Kai	
Lizhi Hong	荔枝紅	Lai Chee Hong	Lichee Black
Longjing	龍井	Lung Tseng	Lung Ching
Lu'an Guapian	六安瓜片	Luk On Ga Pin	
Lushan Yunwu	廬山雲霧	Lo Shaan Wan Mo	

Pinyin	Character	Cantonese	Market Name
Meigui Hongcha	玫瑰紅茶	Mai Kwoi Hang Cha	Rose Congou
Mengding	蒙頂茶	Mung Ding	
Moli Huacha	茉莉花茶	Moot Lei Fa	Jasmine
Pingshui Zhucha	平水珠茶	Ping Sui Chue Cha	Gunpowder
Pu'er	普洱	Po Nei	Pu-erh, Puer
Putuo Fo Cha	普陀佛茶	Po Toh Fat Cha	
Qiangang Huibai	前崗輝白	Chin Gong Foi Bok	
Qihong	祁紅	Kei Hong	Keemun
Shuixian	水仙	Shui Sin	Shui Hsien
Taiping Houkui	太平猴魁	Tai Ping Hau Fui	
Tianmu Qingding	天目青頂	Tin Muk Tsing Ting	
Tie Guanyin	鐵觀音	Tit Koon Yam	Ti Kwan Yin
Tunlu	屯綠	Tin Luk	Tunxi Green
Weishan Maojian	溈山毛尖	Kwoi Shan Mo Jim	

Pinyin	Character	Cantonese	Market Name
Wuyuan Mingmei	婺源名梅	Mo Yuen Ming Mui	
Xinyang Maojian	信陽毛尖	Suen Yueng Mo Jim	
Xishan	西山	Sai Shaan	
Yinfeng	英紅	Ngan Fung	
Yinghong	銀鋒	Ying Hung	Yingteh Black
Yinzhen	銀針	Ngam Jam	
Yongxi Huoqing	涌溪火青	Yung Kai Foh Ching	
Yuhua	雨花	Yue Fa	
Yulu	玉露	Yuk Lo	
Zhengshan Xiaozhong	正山小種	Cheng Shaan Siu Chung	Lapsang Souchong
Zhenmei	珍眉	Jan Mei	
Zisun	紫筍茶	Tsz Sun	

Glossary of Terms

Below are a number of terms, both old and new, that one may encounter in connection with tea, including some names not in our regular Chinese listing.

It should be noted that for promotion purposes, many non-Chinese companies borrow names from Chinese teas, such as Bohea, Congou, Hyson, Souchong, Chunmee, Sowmee, Pekoe, Keemun, etc. Such labels may contain little or no tea of Chinese origin.

Assam　Tea produced in Assam, in northern India. The most poetic description we have heard comes from Michael Spillane, manager of the G. S. Haly Co., tea importers of Redwood City, California. He calls it a bold, dark beverage, almost viscous, like cream, a "round" cup, a heavy beverage with no bite like Darjeeling. It is the base for Irish Breakfast Tea.

Bohea　From Wuyi, the name of a range of mountains that run along the western border of Fujian province. The Dutch were the first to bring to Europe Chinese tea which they got in Java. This tea's name was probably prefaced by its place of origin, as it is today, so when "Wuyi . . . tea" was introduced to Europe, the name carried over—in this form. Originally Bohea (rhymes with Little Mohee) referred to high-grade black tea from Fujian. Later it came to mean a lesser grade of black. The term is rarely used today.

Broken Grade　The leaves have been crushed under a roller into smaller pieces, usually sold in tea bags. They yield their flavor more quickly than full-size leaves.

Caravan   Blend of Chinese Lapsang Souchong and Indian black tea, used only by non-Chinese.

Chrysanthemum Tea   This is the only non-*Camellia* "tea" we list. It is included because it is sold by tea exporters and frequently associated with tea. It consists entirely of the pale yellow blossoms dried and infused like tea. The book *Chinese Medicinal Herbs* lists numerous pharmacological uses.

Congou   Pronounced "kongoo" in the United States. From the Chinese word *gongfu* (*kungfu*, also the English transliteration of the term for martial arts). It is a general name for all non-broken black Chinese teas, though many people now use the term for broken black tea as well. As a tea brewing term, it means "art of tea brewing."

Country Greens   An old non-Chinese designation for all Chinese green tea other than from Huzhou and Pingshui, in Zhejiang province. Used today it may mean any Chinese green. One brand exported from Shanghai uses this name for Young Chunmee.

Darjeeling   A type of Indian black tea made from a small-leafed variety that grows at Darjeeling in the mountainous region of northern India. Sometimes called the champagne of teas, though Chinese Keemun black is often cited as a competitor.

De-enzyme   To deactivate enzymes by steaming, pan-frying, or baking to halt oxidation and remove the source of the raw green taste in tea.

Dust   The finest siftings.

Earl Grey   Many people enjoy this tea without realizing that it represents a moment of British-Chinese friendship in the otherwise hostile century of the Opium War. This blend of India and China blacks gets its unusual flavor from oil of bergamot, made from the peel of the Canton orange *(Citrus aurantium)*. Blossoms of this fruit are used to scent a tea called Tai Tai. What is called the legend of Earl Grey (we were unable to verify details) is that a packet of it and the recipe were given to Charles Grey, the second Earl Grey, when he was British prime minister (1830–1834) as a token of appreciation after a diplomatic mission to China. A Chinese official receiving them was in danger and a member of the British group had saved his life. The earl had this tea made in England for his use, and much later the family allowed it to be made for public sale. It is now marketed by several companies. Twinings claim it as their biggest seller. This tea is not widely consumed in China or by overseas Chinese.

English Breakfast   Originally applied to Chinese black tea in the United States (Ukers), and now includes several blends in which the Chinese flavor predominates. Another view: originally Keemun, later any Chinese black (Blofeld). Today it can also be a combination of Indian and Ceylon teas. In short, a blend of black tea.

Firing   One method of drying or moisture removal in a basket or metal pot using direct heat.

Hyson   A name once widely used for a Chinese green tea. Chinese sources say it comes from *Xi chun* meaning (Kang) *Xi* Spring (Flourishing Spring) and originally referred to the pellet tea (known as Gunpowder in English) which was sent as tribute to Emperor Kang Xi (r. 1661–1722) and also exported. Later this name came to be associated in the export trade with a completely different type of long, tightly rolled leaf produced in Chun'an county, Zhejiang province (see Jiukeng) One version is that this tea was named for the importer who first brought it to Britain, and indeed a cartoon printed in 1755 pictures the shop of the Philip Hyson company, now extinct. The confusion is further compounded by non-Chinese declarations that Hyson comes from the Chinese *yuqian* ("before the rain") but this is unlikely, as many teas have a "before the rain" grade, which simply means the earliest, most tender leaves.

Irish Breakfast   This drink, which has a malt flavor, is so thick that it has a whitish color that looks as if milk has been added. As it cools down, the tannin and caffeine sink to the bottom and a milky film rises to the top. This is called "creaming down."

Lapsang Souchong   Fujian black tea given a smoky flavor through processing with smoke. The name is derived from Zhengshan Xiaozhong, meaning "Sub-variety" (Xiaozhong) of Genuine Wuyi Mountain (Zhengshan) tea.

Mei (Mee) or Eyebrow Teas   The processed leaves of several famous green teas derive their name from the fact that they are eyebrow shaped. These include: *Chunmee* (also *Chunmei* and really *Zhenmei*, Precious Eyebrow) from Zhejiang province; also the highest grades of Tunlu from Anhui province and a twentieth century name in Europe for all Tunlu); *Showmee* (Shoumei, Longevity Eyebrow) Fujian province; *Sowmee* (*Xiumei*, Elegant Eyebrow). A name for teas produced in both Anhui and Zhejiang. *Xiumei* (Beautiful Eyebrow). Another Tunlu tea.

Ming Qian Cha   Tea picked before Qingming Festival, in early April. Any tea picked around this time is supposed to have a high quality. Therefore, the term has come to mean "good quality tea."

Panfiring or firing   The process of drying the leaves by heating them.

Pan-fry   To stir-fry on a large pan, often flat, for the purpose of shaping the leaves and drying them. For famous high-grade teas with a special appearance the tea makers use great skill in shaping the leaves.

Pekoe   From *pek-ho* or *baihao*, the white down which covers certain kinds of leaves and buds. Now it means only two-leaf-one-bud sets sifted to a certain size, and is not a guide to quality. There are also orange pekoe (slightly larger) and flowery orange pekoe, with a lot of tip, or buds. Long ago the name did refer to tea scented with orange blossoms, but now it merely describes a certain appearance.

Pingsuey (Pronounced "pingsooey" when used in English.) Pingshui is a town in Zhejiang province. More than one kind of tea comes prefixed with this name, and "the Pingsueys" is a large general category including several teas from the area. In the United States, teas retailed as Pingsuey are black, although in fact only 10 percent of the Pingshui production is black, and the rest is green. The most famous Pingshui tea is the green Gunpowder.

Rolling   Rolling the tea leaves into tight strips done during pan-frying.

Twankay   Tea books in English list a number of kinds and grades of tea by names that grew up in the nineteenth century based on local pronunciation, or foreign tea buyers' mispronunciation of local place names. Our Chinese tea material takes no note of these. Whether or not they mean something to Western wholesale buyers, they are rarely used for retail sale today, so hardly pertinent to our list. Out of curiosity we investigated this one.

Twankay is a green tea named, according to one source, for two rivers spelled as Taung and Kei (not Chinese pinyin spelling; perhaps the latter is Qi) in the vicinity of the Xinanjiang River near the meeting place of Anhui and Zhejiang provinces. They are too small to be noted in an atlas. The town of Tunxi stands at the convergence of two tributaries of the Xinanjiang. Can Twankay be Tunxi Green?

Young Hyson   See Hyson above. Used only occasionally today for Chinese green tea, and means the younger, more tender leaves.

Yunwu Tea   Several Yunwu (Cloud and Mist) green teas are produced in various parts of China. The name, referring to conditions that produce extremely tender leaves, indicates it is a high-grade tea. They include: Huading Yunwu, also known as Tiantai Yunwu, from Zhejiang and Lushan Yunwu, from Sichuan.

For Further Reading: A Selective Bibliography

Blofeld, John. *The Chinese Art of Tea* (Boston: Shambala, 1985). Highly personalized Taoist-oriented account of history and lore, rare and legendary teas including specials from Taiwan, description of kung-fu *(gongfu)* tea-making, his translations of Chinese Tang and Song tea poems, a chapter on his travels through teahouses of China in the thirties, and excerpts from the tea book by Song dynasty Emperor Hui Cong.

Etherington, Dan M., and Forster, Keith. "The Complex Case of the Chinese Tea Industry." *Food Research Institute Studies* (Food Research Institute of Stanford University), vol. 21, no.3, 1989. The most exhaustive study we have found in English on the Chinese tea industry, recent development, problems, and prospects using figures from Chinese and international sources.

Israel, Andrea. *Taking Tea, The Essential Guide to Brewing, Serving, and Entertaining with Teas from Around the World* (New York: Weidenfeld & Nicholson, 1987). A recent one of many like it with lore, recipes, and a reasonably current list of some of the mail order sellers.

Lu Yu. *The Classic of Tea*, trans., with introduction by Francis Ross Carpenter (Boston: Little, Brown & Co., 1974).

Maitland, Derek. *5000 Years of Tea, a Pictorial Companion* (Hongkong: CFW Publications, Ltd., 1983). Delightful coffee table book.

Okakura, Kakuzo. *The Book of Tea* (New York: Dover Publications, 1964).

Pratt, James Norwood. *The Tea Lover's Treasury* (San Francisco: 101 Productions, 1982). Good on social history in Europe and the coffee-house tea trade. Directory, history of tea firms, ten-page chronology.

Schapira, Joel, David, and Karl. *The Book of Coffee and Tea* (New York: St. Martin's Press, 1975). By members of a tea-coffee merchant family. Section on herbal teas.

Scott, J. M. *The Great Tea Venture* (New York: E. P. Dutton & Co., 1964).

Shalleck, Jamie. *Tea* (New York: The Viking Press, 1972). One of the best on the history of tea in the West. Contains the author's translations of tea descriptions by early Western travelers.

Ukers, William. *All About Tea* (Whitestone, New York: Tea & Coffee Trade Journal Co., 1935). Encyclopedic two-volume collection of information about tea, its history, and the trade as they stood at that time, but now out of date. Quotes of tea in early literature (Chinese, Japanese, English). A basic source for books about tea, including this one.

Ukers, William H. *The Romance of Tea* (New York: Knopf, 1936). A summary of the cultural parts, from his larger two-volume work. Chapter 5, "Tea and the Fine Arts," is a delightful survey of tea in Western art and English literature.

Woodward, Nancy Hyden. *Teas of the World* (New York: Collier Books, Macmillan, 1980). An excellent short history of tea in England and the United States, although her information its background in China is not reliable. Entertaining collection of quotes and verses on tea. Some recipes, tea mail order addresses.

On Related Subjects

Atterbury, Paul, ed. *The History of Porcelain* (New York: Wm. Morrow and Company, Inc., 1982). We are indebted to articles by various writers in this extremely informational and well-written book for much material in chapter eight.

Gaston, Mary Frank. *Blue Willow, An Identification and Value Guide* (Paducah, Ky.: Collector Books, Schroeder Publishing Co. Inc., 1983).

Leung, Albert Y. *Chinese Herbal Remedies* (New York: Universe Books, 1984).

Li Shizhen. *Chinese Medicinal Herbs* (Pencao kangmu), trans. by F. Porter Smith, M.D. and G. A. Stuart, M.D. (San Francisco: Georgetown Press, 1973). A translation of the 1578 classic referred to in this book's text as *Canon of Medicinal Herbs.*

Lo, K. S. *The Stonewares of Yixing from the Ming Period to the Present Day* (Hongkong: Sotheby's Publications and Hongkong University Press, 1987).

Medley, Margaret. *The Chinese Potter: A Practical History of Chinese Ceramics* (Oxford: Phaidon, 1976).

Thomas, Gertrude Z. *Richer than Spices* (New York: Alfred A. Knopf, 1965). Trade and lifestyles that started with the marriage of Portugal's Catherine of Braganza to England's Charles II.

Whipple, A. B. C. *The Clipper Ships* (Alexandria, Virginia: Time-Life Books, 1980).

In Chinese

Tea Research Institute of the Chinese Academy of Agricultural Sciences. *Cha—pinzhi—renlei jiankang guoji xueshu taolun hui, taolun wenzhang gaoyao* (Tea, Quality and Human Health, International Scholarly Symposium, Papers Presented, November 4–9, 1987) Hangzhou, 1988.

Zhuang Wanfang, Tang Qingzhong, Tang Li-xing, Chen Wen Huai and Wang Jiabin. *Zhongguo mingcha* (Famous Teas of China) (Hangzhou: Zhejiang People's Publishing House, 1979).

CHINA BOOKS
FOR ALL THE BEST BOOKS ON CHINA

fig. 1   fig. 2

fig. 3   fig. 4

fig. 5   fig. 6

A Taoist Guide to Longevity

- Qigong
- Movement
- Massage

by Bian Zhizhong

A TAOIST GUIDE TO LONGEVITY
by Bian Zhizhong

Breaking the code of silence imposed on students of Taoism, Bian Zhizhong reveals age-old non-strenuous exercises for the promotion of health, longevity and improved sexual functioning. Large type and fully illustrated instructions make practice easy, and the specific health benefits of each exercise are described in detail.

#2277-8   70 pages   paper $12.95

EASY TAO
by Simon Chang & Fritz Pokorny

These 20 basic exercises, fully illustrated, introduce the ancient Chinese art of health and relaxation known as "Qigong." Beautiful photographs of "regular folks" doing these exercises make these easy-to-hold postures easy to learn. Beneficial for people of all ages, these exercises promote efficiency and fitness, and lead to a balanced and relaxed awareness of life.

#1833-9   160 pages   paper $12.95